Let it Snow

KEEPING CANADA'S WINTER SPORTS ALIVE

DARRYL HUMBER & WILLIAM HUMBER
Foreword by Mayor Hazel McCallion

NATURAL HERITAGE BOOKS
A MEMBER OF THE DUNDURN GROUP
TORONTO

Edited by Jane Gibson
Copy-edited by Shannon Whibbs
Designed by Courtney Horner
Printed and bound in Canada by Marquis

Library and Archives Canada Cataloguing in Publication

Humber, Darryl
        Let it snow : keeping Canada's winter sports
alive / by Darryl Humber and William Humber.

Includes bibliographical references and index.
ISBN 978-1-55488-461-2

        1. Winter sports--Canada. 2. Climatic changes--Canada.
I. Humber, William, 1949- II. Title.

GV840.7.C2H86 2009   796.90971   C2009-903003-9

1   2   3   4   5   13   12   11   10   09

We acknowledge the support of The Canada Council for the Arts and the Ontario Arts Council for our publishing program. We also acknowledge the financial support of the Government of Canada through the Book Publishing Industry Development Program and The Association for the Export of Canadian Books, and the Government of Ontario through the Ontario Book Publishers Tax Credit program, and the Ontario Media Development Corporation.

www.dundurn.com
Published by Natural Heritage Books
A Member of The Dundurn Group

Front cover image © Ben Heys/ iStockphoto
Back cover images: (top) Unidentified group of snowshoers, circa 1914. Manitoba Archives, Foote Collection N2175.
(bottom) "Canadian Winter Sports: A Ladies' Hockey Team, Toronto, Canada." Author's collection

Dundurn Press	Gazelle Book Services Limited	Dundurn Press
3 Church Street, Suite 500	White Cross Mills	2250 Military Road
Toronto, Ontario, Canada	High Town, Lancaster, England	Tonawanda, NY
M5E 1M2	LA1 4XS	U.S.A. 14150

Let it snow

KEEPING CANADA'S WINTER SPORTS ALIVE

TABLE OF CONTENTS

FOREWORD

by Hazel McCallion, C.M.

I have been Mayor of the City of Mississauga, Canada's sixth-largest city and Ontario's third largest, for over thirty years and am well aware of the ways in which our patterns of urban growth have had an effect not only on our quality of life, but conditions, like the weather, we take for granted.

As a young girl growing up in Quebec, I enjoyed the winter months when we counted on snowfalls and freezing nights to make the ice strong for skating and the hills alive with the sound of toboggans.

Those winters made it possible for me to eventually play professional women's hockey in Montreal, though my salary of five dollars a game might not turn too many heads today.

However, we can't be certain any longer about what kind of winter we might get — some have lots of snow, others barely a flake. But we're beginning to understand that the places in which we live have an impact on our climate. The long-term prognosis of many experts isn't encouraging. It would be sad indeed if the Winter Olympics in Vancouver 2010 was the last time we could hold outdoor winter events in Canada because of the season's unpredictability.

Historically, Mississauga started out as a bedroom community with many of the conditions we now associate with urban sprawl. I wish now that more attention had been given to higher-density or transit-supportive land uses along our arterial roads. We are now trying to reverse some of the worst aspects of sprawl, and in so doing, contribute to the reduction in factors causing global warming.

These measures include providing more local employment opportunities, enhancing our natural areas, establishing a more compact and efficient urban form that supports transit, and improving the quality of our built environment and the unique character of our communities.

Mississauga is aware of the ability of trees to mitigate the impacts of climate change. It has also discovered first-hand the impacts of more extreme weather on tree health and increased tree damage. The City,

Photo Courtesy of The Mississauga News/Rob Beintema. Special thanks to Maureen Ellis and Carol Horvat, the City of Mississauga.

under its Strategic Plan, has established ambitious targets to increase tree cover and will, in the future, select tree species with the potential impacts of climate change and invasive insects in mind.

I myself continue to skate and enjoy our winter conditions, but as I do, I am mindful of the duty we all have to ensure that future generations will experience the same magnificent enjoyment of this splendid season.

I welcome Darryl and William Humber's book, which is not only sounding an alarm about the threat to our outdoor winter sports, but also reminding us how joyful those activities continue to be. Theirs is a message of hope that something can be done to ensure winter's long-term health.

The people in Mississauga are trying to do their part to keep the ice frozen and the hills alive with the sound of toboggans. I have no plans to pack my skates away anytime soon!

Hazel McCallion, C.M.
Mayor

ACKNOWLEDGEMENTS

We begin by thanking the folks at Dundurn Press and Jane Gibson and Barry Penhale in particular. Their imprint, Natural Heritage Books, is now part of a significant Canadian publishing presence. These are challenging times for the makers of books and hopefully we are, in our small way by investing countless hours in research and writing, doing our part to keep this miracle of human culture alive and thriving.

This is Darryl's first work of non-fiction, having completed two works of fiction in the last four years. For Bill, (or William, as he prefers his byline to read) it is his eleventh. Past efforts have included those on baseball, soccer, and bicycling, and two with Natural Heritage, one on both Darryl and Bill's hometown, Bowmanville, Ontario, and the other on African-Canadian athletes.

We salute the patience and help of many, including Darryl and Bill's family members — mother/wife Cathie, brother/son Brad, sister/daughter Karen, uncle/brother Larry (whose art designs were wonderful), aunt/ sister Mary, grandmother/mother-in-law Ruth, and for Darryl, Ann-Marie Gazley, who also chipped in with research support.

For making this book possible, we thank the brilliant graphic artist Aleks Janicijevic, the escapee from London's February 2009 winter surprise Leeroy Murray, the proofreading brilliance and critical comments of Sally Moore, Todd Latham, and Suzanne Elston. Resources and research were provided by the dean of hockey researchers, Bill Fitsell, and another Society for International Hockey Research stalwart, Martin Harris.

Colleagues at Seneca with whom Bill works on matters related to climate change include Mary Dawson, Roy Paluoja, Gary Johnson, Carolyn Anderson, Steve Wilson, Ken Ellis, and countless others who will torment him with cries of, "Why didn't you mention me?"

We dedicate this book to the memory of Alfred Humber, the grandfather/father of Darryl and Bill, in recognition of his long nights of backyard ice-making. Neither he nor the mysterious lady in our introduction who befriended Joseph Atkinson could have known they would find their way into a book so many years later. The good they did, however, lives forever and this is its small reward.

INTRODUCTION

The following story might be apocryphal, but one hopes it is true.

Joseph E. Atkinson began his career as a journalist and rose to become publisher of the *Toronto Star*, from which he developed a reputation as a reformer and defender of the less fortunate. Born near Newcastle, Ontario, in 1865, he died in 1948, but the charitable foundation bearing his name continues to do good work over sixty years later.

It does so perhaps because of an incident Atkinson recalled from his boyhood days in Newcastle. He was, by his own description, a small and fragile lad with a speech impediment lasting into his twenties.

"I was sitting at the edge of the village pond, watching the skating. My brothers and sisters and my playmates were having a furious time. It didn't occur to me to ask for or even expect skates. In families such as ours not everybody could have a pair. You had to wait for an older brother to outgrow his and pass them on to you.

"I noticed a lady standing off to the side. She asked me why I wasn't skating with the others. I told her, without any sense of envy, that I had no skates. It was one of the natural things about life.

"She took my hand and asked me to come with her. We went into a village store and to my astonishment she bought me a pair of skates.

"'To keep?' I asked her.

'Of course,' she said.

"I went back to the pond in a daze of glory. I never forgot it. And as for the lady, I never saw her again."

Winter is Canada's splendid season and it inspires acts of generosity, from cleaning a neighbour's sidewalk to commiserating with colleagues on a hard day's journey into work. In Bowmanville, very near Atkinson's childhood home in Newcastle, it's the act of Al and Anna Strike building an ice rink on their front lawn for local children to use even though their own grew up and left home years ago. It's a tradition approaching its fiftieth year and this book is at least partly a celebration of dedication such as theirs.

There's a lot of ill-informed commentary about our shared experience of snow and cold somehow making us a hardier, more resilient, and tougher people. It just may be an opposite impact, however, that makes winter so prominent in our history and attitude toward others.

Weather, in this case winter, humbles us with its power and its indifference to our fate. We tamper with it at our peril.

Sports are the means Canadians use to fight back against the harsh reality of the season that informs so many metaphors of decline and death. In sports we triumph or find honour in participation.

From the days Canadians discovered in snowshoeing a sporting element and surrounded it with group songs and mixed hikes, to the steely resolve of curlers on mid-winter outdoor rinks, fortified by their whisky and haggis, and finally to the present day in which youngsters and their parents wake early in the cold and dark for 5:00 a.m. hockey practices, sports isn't just the way we survive winter, it's the way we revel in its opportunities.

Climate change may erode this happy relationship and so it is incumbent on Canadians to lead the way, at first, in reversing this trend and then by restoring the glory of winter. It is a cause for national interest and engagement! Hopefully our words will do their part.

Darryl Humber
William Humber

ONE

Wishing Winter was Nine Months Long: Winter in Canada's Story

Ah, for the days when winter arrived in November and lasted well into April, when snow piled up to the second floor of one's house, and summer was, as they say, two months of bad skating. Or are these just memories we tell each other as we age? Sometimes it seems as if we live in the dream of a world that existed only in our imaginations, like a Canadian version of the "Songlines" guiding the pathways of Australia's original inhabitants.

If you live in western Canada, one such dream might consist of skating on an icy slough, that marshy, or reedy pool, pond, inlet, or backwater near a creek off which youngsters and their parents would shovel snow, perhaps by hand. Hot water drawn from a steam engine used to crush grain during the day might be drained into a few barrels, then placed on a sled and brought down to the creek and dumped onto the ice to help level the surface.

This was no "slough of despair" as described in John Bunyan's *Pilgrim's Progress*, a book that ironically might have sat in the limited library of those Bible-believing skaters. It was a special place in which skates were clamped on one's leather shoes, eventually tearing off the soles. Hockey sticks were fashioned from crooked willow branches and a puck could be anything from a block of wood to a frozen cow pie.

In eastern Canada the dream of winter was more often of the pleasures found in natural rinks built in schoolyards or in one's backyard. Long into the nights youngsters would glide over the glassy surface, drawn home only by the call for dinner.

In Ontario your treasure was most likely a Toronto Maple Leafs sweater. In Quebec youngsters donned the bright *"rouge, blanc et blue"* of *Les Canadiens*, unless, like the unfortunate child in Roch Carrier's "The Hockey Sweater" (*"Le chandail de hockey"*), the T. Eaton Company mistakenly sent the young Quebecker one emblazoned with *"une abominable feuille d'érable"* or "an abominable maple leaf," in which case your mother made you wear it so as not to disappoint Mr. Eaton.

If there is such a thing as a series of small straws that eventually broke the back of national unity, Carrier's fictional character had more than his load, though on a deeper level the story speaks to the profound shared experience of all Canadians, regardless of whether their first language is French of English. Saturday nights in winter were the purest demonstrations of this realm.

If you lived in English Canada, it was a magical time for listening to Foster Hewitt's radio call of the Leafs game. He inspired young and old to imagine their own lives as great stars or at the very least as persons who might one day be lucky enough to spend just one evening in the hallowed Maple Leaf Gardens. It was the closest thing to a public shrine in Canada, that is unless you lived in Quebec, where the Montreal Forum played a similarly haunting role.

Young women might vicariously share in these moments, but for them the exploits of Barbara Ann Scott, women's figure-skating gold medalist in the 1948 Winter Olympics, inspired their own twirls and spins on ice, even as they asked Santa Claus to please leave under their family tree a doll fashioned in the likeness of the great skater who had won her first national junior title as an eleven-year-old.

Winter has shaped Canada's image and been embraced with hearty enthusiasm from snowshoeing hikers in the nineteenth century to future

Simcoe County Archives, Frank Grant Collection.

A Barrie women's hockey team in 1897. Back row: Louise King, Mabel Lowe, Mrs. Ben Smith, Lucie Payne, Flo Brigham, May Graham; front row: Annie Graham, Amy Lowe, Ethel Urquhart.

hockey stars on homemade rinks and to the indoor spectacle of figure-skating carnivals and curling bonspiels.

Our literature, our songs, and our memories of youth all have their connection to winter's refreshing tonic. Even as we curse ice-laden roads on the morning commute to work or watch with keen anticipation the Weather Channel's daily prediction for our weekend ski trip, Canadians sense that somehow this bracing time of year is central to their very survival.

In Montreal, snowshoers of the nineteenth century sang their wish that winter could be nine months long, but alas, twenty-first-century winter's diminishment to a weak reminder of its former glory is a real possibility as climate change wreaks long-term havoc. Winter means something for the sense of Canadian identity, and for the collective memory of the country's heritage, nor should we forget those businesses and industries dependent on the "splendid season."

It's quite possible, however, that Vancouver's hosting of the 2010 Winter Olympics will mark the last time the Games will ever be held in Canada. Assuming Canada is called upon in twenty to twenty-four years from now (the period between the Games in Calgary in 1988 and those in 2010 was twenty-two years because the Games began a new four-year cycle in 1994, two years after those in 1992, in order that they not be held the same year as the Summer Games), winter may be a fading memory, or the cost of moving all events indoors may make them financially prohibitive. We can't forget that hockey, figure skating, and speed skating were all once played on outdoor surfaces.

It isn't that one can't build an indoor facility for ski jumping or any number of outdoor sports. The better question is why one would want to other than as a fading memory of a once noble time of year?

In these pages we embark upon a voyage of both remembrance and caution. Looking back at the conditions that instilled feverish excitement at the first glimpse of a snowflake in the darkening days of late fall, and forward to the unusual world of melting ice caps, unpredictable weather, and assaults on Canada's backyard ice rink culture.

Winter plays a major role in the Canadian story, not only in how it has shaped our sports history, but, more directly, our experience of everyday life. Nor is climate change only to blame for changes in its role. Increasing urbanization and higher expectations of comfort have also played their part in lessening winter's place in our lives.

What did our great grandparents and their predecessors think of winter's distinct conditions? No doubt they griped, but evidence seems to suggest they also welcomed its peculiar opportunities.

Fred Grant's memories from this era, preserved in the Simcoe County Archives outside Barrie, Ontario, provide some clues. Writing in the early 1920s, many years after he had left for the Pacific Coast to play professional lacrosse in Victoria in early 1892, he recalled the winter sports and recreation of his youth in Barrie and its surroundings in the

Simcoe County Archives, Frank Grant Collection.

A Barrie women's hockey team in the early twentieth century. Back row: Bertha Holmes, Del Spry, Georgie Maconchy; front row: Zilla Stevenson, Olive McCarthy, Jessie Oliver, Bessie Stevenson.

1870s and 1880s. He also had many things to say about how games like hockey have morphed into something different in the twentieth century.

He will be an occasional companion as we undertake this journey.

A small community of a few thousand people, approximately one hundred kilometres north of downtown Toronto, Barrie in the late nineteenth century was the gateway to the emerging cottage and summer recreation country north of it, and the main centre for a largely rural hinterland.

Fred Grant's memories of his youth reflected Barrie's countryside location and its position on the shores of Kempenfelt Bay, off Lake Simcoe. It was here he witnessed an unusual sport characteristic of the day:

Horse racing on the ice on Barrie's bay used to be a very popular sport, and was held during a whole week each winter. A mile track, sixty feet or more wide was cleared with a huge snow scraper, and the resulting races provided most interesting sport for the very large crowds of spectators and horsemen from all over the province, as well as the local followers of the sport.

And of course these latter included the curious small boy who always found something interesting in anything new. Sometimes after a ridge of snow three or four feet high on either side of the track had been piled up by the scraper, a thaw and frost would follow, and open-air skating would be carried on, while these races were being run, which added to the enjoyment.

The names of the horses are not so easily remembered, but the popular favourite always was a little black horse that stood straight up on its hind feet and looked as if it would topple over on the driver each time it turned before starting — I think it was named Black Diamond, and it certainly could travel too though it was only half the size of the other racers.

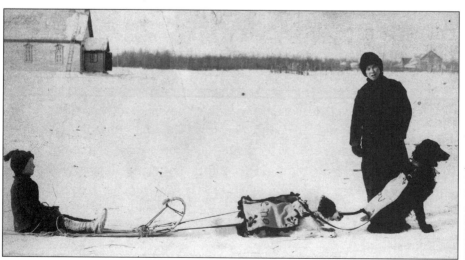

Sledding in Manitoba, 1886.

Manitoba Archives, Dorothy Garbutt Collection 38.

One might ask if a time can be pinpointed when this winter experience of outdoor frivolity and lively socialization disappeared from the everyday, generally positive experience of Canadians and became simply a nuisance to overcome and an aggravation to endure? Or, despite our grumbling, do we not secretly relish the season as one distinctly our own, particularly in the ways we respond to its challenges and revel in its possibilities?

Canadians of the nineteenth century not only watched horse races on ice, but curled on outdoor ponds, and played their first hockey games on natural surfaces subject to fluctuating temperatures. By all accounts citizens of the day accepted such experiences as normal and, in their own way, part of the charm of living in a northern climate. Work was something to which they generally did not commute, particularly if they lived in the countryside. The greatest hazard may have been removing snow from overloaded roofs, getting lost on roads covered in drifting snow, or falling afoul of the era's restrictive social codes.

Recalling those days when young women and men occasionally tested limits to their freedom, Grant said:

> Of all those winter pastimes of boyhood days in Barrie, probably the one with the greatest appeal to those now many years absent from the old town were the skating parties on the bay, especially when the arrival of a clear expanse of ice and a bright moonlit night happened at the same time.
>
> There were many times when the surface of the entire lake was frozen over, and a skate to Big Bay Point and even to Orillia was enjoyed. On one occasion, however, I had the pleasure of being one of a crowd of half-a-dozen couples who, one moonlit night, skated from in front of Barrie station down past Big Bay Point, across a corner of Lake Simcoe to the mouth of the Holland River and up the river to the railroad bridge, half a mile or so south of the Bradford station, and returning on the midnight train, which at that time was the transcontinental one.

It would never do at this late date to mention the girls' names, as some of them are grandmothers now, and besides, we had no chaperone on the trip.

From such a daily engagement with winter on a daily basis, conditions began to change significantly for Canadians in the last part of that century. The growth of large-scale industry and manufacturing in urban centres occurred alongside the associated termination of smaller operations in rural towns. Fixed-link transportation afforded by trains contributed to the centralization of many cultural and sporting activities once distributed over a wider geographic region, while waterfront industries powered by steam power, made big city living an economic powerhouse in which people with higher incomes could purchase consumer goods unimaginable a generation before. The daily press, the department store, theatres, and commercial sports made the city a destination for increasing numbers of rural dwellers.

By the early twentieth century, a further transition was occurring. The private automobile and alternating-current electricity made suburbanization possible as well as the gradual redistribution of industrial production from its downtown locations. All this did, however, was make the city bigger. Its rural counterparts, and their associated memories, grew weaker. There would be no going back to a supposedly "simpler" age.

Meanwhile, in the countryside by the 1880s, improvements in agricultural mechanization and competition from the wheat fields of the West resulted in an almost fifty-year period of rural depopulation, as many in eastern Canada flocked west to take advantage of the virgin farmlands of the prairies.

Fred Grant was one of those, but for him this was a new territory of winter pleasures to explore:

In December 1898, I had the pleasure of being a member of a bunch of hockey players in Golden, B.C., who journeyed to Banff, Alberta, to meet the team of that place in a game on the Bow River, and among the entertainers were four former Barrieites — Mr. and Mrs.

Simcoe Country Archives Negative #646.

Thomas Jebb, a local enthusiast in Orillia at the start of the twentieth century, enjoys the winter weather.

"Bob" Campbell, the former the principal of the public school there, a player on the Banff team, now a resident of Calgary and a member of the Alberta Legislature, and a very pronounced opponent of the party led by his fellow townsman Premier Stewart; Tom Wilson, the owner of a large outfitting business for tourist and mountaineering parties, frequently a guide to Dominion Government Geological parties, and probably the best-informed man in Canada on the famous Lake Louise and Yoho Valley Districts; and Billy Alexander, then and now in the jewellery business.

A whole story could be written about this wonderful national park [Banff] and its many novel attractions from its spray falls and truly wonderful "Cave and "Basin," [Historic Site] where swimming in the open air takes place amid a forty-below-zero temperature and high piles of snow up to the very edge of the pool in which the overflow water from the ever-bubbling warm sulphur springs of "The Cave" makes things comfortable so long as you keep immersed, up to the magnificent CPR Banff Springs Hotel, which seems to be suspended up among the clouds when viewed from the "Valley of the Bow."

Among the many entertaining features provided for the visitor was a sleigh ride through the park, past a big herd of buffalo running loose pretty much as they did in the wild state, and browsing on buds of the young trees and bushes, and many a scurrying coyote who hiked for cover upon approach of humans.

Urbanization by itself was no reason for winter to have a declining role in the daily lives of Canadians, but perhaps in retrospect it was inevitable, at least during the first formative decades of the twentieth century. City homes with central heating were, for all their primitive protection, far more comfortable than country places in which wood-burning heat might only be provided to a few rooms and turned off completely at night.

Quickly lost from memory were the ways in which winter in the country had been a respite from at least some outdoor chores for both adults and children. In the absence of the world of modern media, a young child in particular anticipated the coming winter season as a world exemplified by perfect natural ice on an open pond, or at least according to Fred Grant:

> When the ice was first formed on the ponds or bay, of course it was always some venturesome small boy who was first out. It was impossible to control him when the whole bay was open to him, but when only a small surface was available the town constable — Tom Blain or Jim Marrin or Jimmy Carson — was very conservative about allowing anyone on until it was perfectly safe, though they might be assured, "That ice is strong enough to hold a herd of elephants. When are you going to let us on?"
>
> If everyone would content himself or herself with decorous straight-away skating everything would be satisfactory, but it would require the Arctic Ocean to give safe room for the scooting kids in a game of tag, and a bunch of girls doing a combined figure eight, while some fellow cut a swath the whole width of the pond with his outside edge, or spread-eagle, scissors or smoothing iron; and did you ever see a couple doing the double grapevine who turned out of their course for anyone?
>
> But the most disastrous skating menace was the scorcher with humped shoulders who raced ahead until he met some struggling couple or an earnest exponent of some of the above stunts when there would be a heap of ruins.

Winter, however, was only a minor hindrance to daily employment in the industrial city. Work was no longer necessarily in one's own neighbourhood and usually required travelling on crowded streetcars, or, if one was more fortunate, a poorly insulated private car. City streets

Simcoe County Archives 971-77, Box 34, Vespra.

This photo of John Campbell of Parry Sound, circa 1895, recalls an era when winter was king.

required one's personal labour to be cleared of snow, while icy hazards had to be avoided by wary pedestrians, such as broken bones from falls. Winter, in short, was increasingly a nuisance and not something to be embraced. Indeed for these early city "pioneers" there was likely less engagement in winter sports then for later generations of city dwellers.

Part of this was due to "blue laws" emerging from the Sabbatarian movement in the early decades of the twentieth century. They restricted Sunday activities in many cities so that by 1912 tobogganing was banned in places like Toronto's High Park on the one day that most people might have the leisure time to enjoy it.

Urban poverty, long working hours, and then two wars and a depression ensured that a return to the glory of winter activity similar to that of the countryside past would have to await more affluent lifestyles of the post–Second World War period.

If anything, city dwellers relied on watching others take part in activities they had once participated in themselves. Professional hockey as a modern commercial entertainment played in indoor hockey palaces was perfectly suited to the needs of these city residents. Cities like Montreal and Toronto differentiated themselves from neighbouring pretenders like Ottawa and Hamilton by building increasingly larger arenas, culminating, in the case of Toronto, in the opening of Maple Leaf Gardens in 1931.

So while in bigger cities like Toronto or Montreal, and particularly the newer ones of Calgary and Edmonton, the countryside remained almost within a reasonable walking distance away, it was a place increasingly removed from most city dwellers' daily experience.

Alongside this, the expectation of convenience associated with life in the city suggested to many that even a semblance of discomfort, such as that associated with outdoor winter activity, was something to be abandoned as a remnant of the past.

In Toronto, there would be one last winter to remember the season's pleasures and its challenges before war and urbanization's other demands consigned to memory this older, almost naive pleasure of the season. It occurred even as the seeds were being planted for winter's eventual transition to its modern form as a commodity whose pleasure would

A hockey club from Elmvale, Ontario, undated.

Simcoe County Archives Glass Negative #124.

increasingly be purchased either in the form of hockey equipment from CCM and Eaton's, or weekend skiing getaways, at first to little hills north of the city, but gradually to more remote and expensive resorts.

For CCM, or the Canada Cycle and Motor Company, winter was its corporate salvation.

Formed in the late nineteenth century as a conglomerate of smaller bicycle-making companies to compete with big American importers, the bottom had almost immediately dropped out of the cycling market. Cleverly, its Canadian managers opted for a year-round strategy of producing and selling bikes and accessories in the summer and skates and hockey equipment in the winter.

The irony in CCM's case was that as bankruptcy overtook the company by the 1970s, its most valuable commodity was its logo and brand name, which survives today on hockey sweaters and helmets, and no doubt mystifies users as to its origin.

To our contemporary senses the long-ago winter of 1912 was as miserable as could be — so cold that by the end of February, Lake Ontario had frozen over and citizens wandered kilometres out into the lake to catch a glimpse of Rochester. Temperatures fell below -10°C on 56 days, while snowfall at 1.43 metres was nearly double the normal.

Trees and ice on the lake exploded in the cold with a sound like gunfire, the airbrakes of streetcars froze, and natural gas lines were clogged in a solid mass that had to be continually pumped. One simply bundled up against its worst sting and school went on despite the need to wear one's outdoor clothing in rooms often no more than 18°C.

But the ice sailing in Toronto harbour was brilliant, and the early challenges of artificial ice were forgotten for at least one winter.

If he hadn't moved west by this time Fred Grant might have joined the festivities, as he recalled his own youth in Barrie:

> There used to be some pretty fine sport, too, in ice-boating on the bay, in which Levi Carley and Ike Boon were the most prominent and had the fastest and largest boats. It was fun enough when you were out skating to jump on and have a ride, but far better to hang onto the frame and

slide on your skates, and when it came to the boat making a sharp turn, why "crack-the-whip" wasn't in it with the flip you'd get, and it was entirely your own affair whether you slid away on your skates or on the back of your neck.

Of course, you remember the old slide you had sprinkled and then polished up until it was just about the slipperiest spot in town — and usually right in the path of the greatest pedestrian traffic (and if it had a slant, so much the better, as it was easier to keep going once you got started) and then some old curmudgeon would come along with a can of ashes and spoil the whole shooting-match, with the curt admonition, "What's the matter with you kids; do you want to break your bloomin' necks?" And who never paid any attention to your very pertinent rejoinder, "We wasn't hurtin' anything; guess they are our own necks, ain't they?"

Some activities like ice boating eventually did disappear while others like tobogganing became the property only of children. The hardships of the winter of 1912 were quickly forgotten as people got on with life in the big cities of the land.

In a few short years young men would be off to a war from which many would never return, and for survivors those lost years were in many cases made up by finally turning their backs on that residue of memory of seasonal discomfort that their parents, grandparents, and themselves as children had once embraced.

Fred Grant recalled what had been lost:

Those old sleighing parties provided many an evening's happy enjoyment. Their objective was usually out into the country to some farmer's home, where part of the evening would be spent in a social dance, or "parlour games" in the case of younger people making up the party, and to "thawing out" before taking the couple of hours return trip.

West Street Rink in Orillia during the 1880s.

The box of the commodious old sleigh had been filled a foot or so deep with straw, and robes and blankets galore provided when the weather was really cold and the driving snow bit into a fellow's cheeks. But in the sleigh days and nights no one was afraid of blizzards. Having got out into the country, many times the roads were found impassable through the drifts and a shortcut would be taken through the fields, and lots of times was the snowfall so heavy that it covered up the rail fences, and when it didn't as many of the top rails as necessary would be removed to allow a passage.

Later on we were old enough to pilot a single rig ourselves. They talk now of a motor spark plug, meaning a second-hand "tin lizzie" probably, but ask any of the old boys and they'll tell you they had nothing on an old-fashioned horse and cutter outfit you could hire for two dollars for a whole afternoon or evening at Alex Fraser's Livery.

Two wars and a depression didn't kill the experience of winter, but did consign it to a place of less prominence in daily lives. It would take the return of a somewhat more stable peace after 1945, and the increasing affluence of this post–Second World War period to finally restart the great engine of winter sports.

At first it was youngsters playing hockey in an expanding network of minor hockey in the 1950s. However, it was an enthusiasm generally available only for boys, although one young girl named Abby Hoffman did make an improvised appearance on one of those gender-limiting teams before her eventual discovery.

There was the steady growth of a winter-sports industry for skiers and curlers in an expanding network of clubs and resorts. Once formerly limited to only the very wealthy, these sports now attracted a more egalitarian membership.

Adventurous baby boomers who came of age as teenagers in the 1960s discovered there was more to life than their stereotyped existence of sex, drugs, and rock and roll by popularizing entirely new recreations like snowboarding and freestyle skiing. Less frantic members of this age group opted for cross-country skiing, which enjoyed an extraordinary boom in the 1970s.

Within a few years a society that had only recently rejected the playing wishes of young girls like Abby Hoffman had been completely transformed. By the 1990s organized women's hockey was flourishing.

For those who thought they had left that part of their lives behind, senior men's hockey challenged the already overstretched schedules of local hockey rinks. When some of their fellow players succumbed to heart attacks on ice, their friends rationalized that at least they died doing something they liked, and then kept right on playing, their own mortality hanging in some cases by the same fragile encounter with full time.

The growth of year-round lifestyle communities in places like Whistler, British Columbia, or Collingwood, Ontario, completed the re-entry of winter into the lives of Canadians, though its residents must have sufficient

Glenbow Alberta Institute, Bill Fitsell Collection NA-1758-17.

Hockey on frozen slough, east of Viking, Alberta, 1912.

resources to live there. It is the enjoyment of the lifestyle associated with those places, which ironically is now part of the larger dilemma we face in ensuring the continuance of future winter conditions.

Winter has now become more than a season. It is a window into the future. It is reflected on an almost daily basis in the glaciers and ice fields and snow-packed mountains and backyard rinks and even the permafrost in Arctic wilderness, and the penguins and polar bears that live in the dark and cold places of the world.

Climate change, once the topic of mild concern, and then intense debate, is now acknowledged to be an increasing threat to survival, or at least to our ability to live within reasonably tolerant levels of heat and frost.

How we deal with that challenge will define our place in the world for centuries, and along with that, a world in which winter is commonplace rather than a rare experience. Human willingness to confront this challenge is at least partly based on our ability to look back at what once so enflamed passions and created a distinct national identity.

It is easy to forget the glories of what once was, and instead take for granted as both inevitable and normal, our experience of the world today and into the future.

Winter, the "splendid season," is more than just a time of year. It is the metaphor of who and what Canadians have been, are, and imagine themselves to be. Winning gold medals or owning the podium at the 2010 Winter Olympics in Vancouver would only be a shallow victory if Canadians accepted winter's decline as a fact of life beyond their control.

TWO

How Winter Has Shaped Canadian Identity from Literature to Art

What is a Canadian? It's an open-ended question that inevitably generates as many answers as there are people considering it. Responses have changed over the years, as Canadian identity has shifted throughout the decades.

One of the more recent ways of describing a Canadian, however, is contrasting the differences between them and their influential neighbours directly to the south. If you continue that dialogue though, eventually and inevitably, the conversation reverts to a time-honoured self-identifier. Pressed hard enough, most will declare it is a Canadian's relationship with winter. Snow, sleet, blinding blizzards, and ice are all symbols of the Canadian experience, and the telling images of who we are.

Winter is not simply one of four seasons to a Canadian. It's not merely the time separating fall from the spring. It's much more. Winter in Canada is a force. Its power has made Canadians who they are, in the same way the Declaration of Independence defines Americans and soccer-playing connotes the Brazilians. It's what we're known for whether we like it or not. Take winter away and would we still be Canadians?

Perhaps our own self-image would adjust, but the rest of the world might have trouble responding to this lost cliché.

Robertson Davies claimed that "cold breeds caution," suggesting not too subtly the relationship between the winter climate and the psyche of Canadians as a whole. Canada is in a winterized state for a major part of the calendar year. In certain areas of Canada, winter is extreme, debilitating, and fierce. The calendar definition of the season running from just before Christmas through late March is one of the more misleading markers. Davies argues that because of the cold climate Canadians are perhaps more cynical and paranoid. This receives added credence in the way it contributes to the Canadian desire to separate themselves from Americans.

The blending of American and Canadian cultures has become more pronounced in recent years. Canadians are offended by this development and rely on critical sustenance for their ability to differentiate themselves from Americans by virtue of being winter warriors.

This bond between Canada and winter is best described by French-Canadian singer Gilles Vigneault, who succinctly remarked, "My country's not a country, it's winter." His country, however, was not necessarily Canada. It is symptomatic of the complex nature of Canadian identity that Vigneault is described as a poet, publisher, singer-songwriter, and well-known Quebec nationalist and sovereignist.

So, no sooner do Canadians find an artist who expresses his people's attitude to their relationship with winter then he disavows his interest in such an identity.

Still, Canadians wear this relationship between themselves and climate as a badge of honour. Canadians travelling abroad check into international hostels with maple leaves attached to their backpacks and proudly tell a traveller from Spain, "If I can take a Canadian winter, I can certainly rough it in this hostel." The Canadian then proudly annoys his indifferent host by describing his survival of major snowfalls. His host, on the other hand, wonders why he can find nothing to say about Canada's cuisine or its major musical artists.

Canadians have no choice. They embrace the frigid winters as something that makes them unique. Blinding snow, extreme windchill,

Manitoba Archives.

Horse racing on a frozen river.

freezing rain, and blizzards are hazards they tolerate every year, something that is foreign to the majority of other countries. A Canadian traveller would be at a loss if someone checked into the same hostel and was from Iceland. They would feel somewhat emasculated.

American comedic writer Dave Barry famously wrote: "The problem with winter sports is that — follow me closely here — they generally take place in winter." Canadians, however, embrace winter sports because for far too many months there simply is no other choice.

Of course, a Canadian could declare a disaffection with the season and many do by fleeing south during its harsher months, but in so doing there's a sneaking suspicion that they must be less than a "real Canadian." Winter culture surrounds Canadians, telling them that hockey, snowmobiling, and ice fishing are their activities. Basketball may have been created by a Canadian, but being a basketball fan does not make you a Canadian. Basketball is now too connected with American culture to qualify as Canadian.

Canadians must embrace their sports to be truly genuine, and they do, but, of course, with a caveat that it is what is expected of them. The outsider will quickly know they are in Canada once they turn on a television and investigate the country's sports stations. Two will be showing hockey games, a third will have aging veterans of the game talking about hockey games and prattling on about how necessary fighting is to the game's definition, while a fourth station will be showing a curling match.

Those from other countries are of course baffled by this strange cultural abnormality. A caller to a Geneva, Switzerland, sports talk show in the year 2000, having spent some time in Canada watching television, inquired of the bemused host whether Canadian parents, as a rite of passage for children, removed all their child's front teeth before putting them into the game as the loss was inevitable in any case. The host was unable to contradict this apparent European urban myth.

The most promising basketball tandem in Toronto in the early twenty-first century, featuring the mercurial Vince Carter and his cousin Tracy McGrady, was broken up by McGrady's protest that he needed to get out of Canada because not only was the American sports station ESPN not available but its alternative, TSN, only covered curling — hour after hour of Vic Rauter proclaiming the mystery of draws, and rocks, and buttons, which McGrady found culturally baffling. The promise of a National Basketball Association dynasty in Toronto was thus shattered by the country's bizarre winter sports fixation.

From childhood, young boys in the long winters have little choice but to embrace the games of ice and snow. There are few facilities that can accommodate children playing football or baseball indoors during the long winter months, so thousands of children travel to the closest rink, or to a frozen pond or homemade rink, and join their friends.

It's an upbringing that is unavoidable. The relationship between Canadians and the winter has created a culture that almost exclusively holds winter events as the defining moments in the country's sports history. Some of the best-defined cultural events of the past fifty years have involved the game of hockey. Arguably none was more significant than Paul Henderson's goal to win the Summit Series with Russia (okay, they called themselves the Soviet Union, but to Canadians they were Russians) in 1972. Canadians also recall the collective joy of the nation following Mario Lemieux's goal for Team Canada in 1987 in the penultimate match with those same Russians.

Hockey defines Canadians so much now that politicians use the winter sport as a benchmark to create new legislation.

One has only to consider a proposed Federal holiday brought forward in February 2009 by Linda Duncan, an Edmonton MP. In her proposal, Duncan argued that the third Friday of February be declared, as one might have already guessed, "Hockey Day."

Duncan's proposal, not surprisingly, was quick fodder for the national media. Any story involving hockey and politics gets the attention of Canadians. Its presence on websites inspired a flurry of comments and sparked vigorous debates from Canadians throughout the nation. Some comments by Canadians online spoke directly to the state of Canada's culture. Some wondered how Canadians have got to the point where the nation, once joked about as being a hockey-playing, beer-drinking, parka-wearing fraternity, now had politicians proposing holidays directly catering to some of these oversimplifications. Had we become a country requiring a holiday to tell us what we already knew to be our story? Duncan defended her proposal, saying, "Hockey has served as a unifying force throughout our history and it is a significant facet of our national identity."

Duncan tapped into a distinctly Canadian myth that we are somehow uniquely strong and capable of living with, and even prospering in, long winters, as opposed to the easier ability of people in warmer climates to address their challenges. The holiday would help ease the Canadian difficulty in surviving long, harsh winters.

"People need days off in the winter to fight the blues, and what better holiday could there be than one that would celebrate our national game?" Duncan explained.

This is not a new concept. Winter has been a major influence on the comments and actions of prominent Canadian statesmen and politicians. In 1866, Nova Scotia statesman Joseph Howe cheekily viewed Canada as not being able to fully loosen its shackles.

"[We] may be pardoned if we prefer London under the Dominion of John Bull to Ottawa under the domination of Jack Frost," he remarked.

Prominent politicians, like popular Prime Minister Pierre Trudeau, also noted Canada's relationship with its unique weather patterns. "Canada is a country whose main exports are hockey players and cold fronts. Our main imports are baseball players and acid rain," he said.

A curling team sponsored by Sangster, circa 1915.

Manitoba Archives, Foote Collection N7407.

Trudeau's political counterpart, conservative politician Joe Clark, joined the fray of characterizing Canada as a winter wonderland in his description of Canada as "The Winter half of North America."

Politicians seemingly have no problem creating sound bites signifying a long-standing overexaggeration of Canada's climate, even if their comments don't necessarily apply to the majority of Canadians who live in somewhat more temperate regions of the country.

Generalizing Canada's identity as a winter nation has its roots in the ways Canadians define their country. While cold winters certainly affect northern Canada, and cities such as Edmonton or Calgary, frosty, unbearable winters are not as applicable to residents of Windsor, Toronto, and Vancouver, which contain the majority of Canadians.

Torontonians share a climate similar to Buffalo, New York (but with less snow), and Detroit (but with less laid-off auto workers) for the majority of the year. Being Canadian, however, allows them to travel abroad and proudly declare that they are like winter soldiers who are able to endure the roughest of Canadian winters, while reassuring southerners, tongue firmly planted in cheek, that they don't live in igloos, as their new house was built with bricks and mortar.

It's a misconception of sorts that Canadians love to exploit in the manner of people who have lived so long with an ironic self-image they now believe it to be fact. Rick Mercer, a popular Canadian CBC (Canadian Broadcasting Company) comic, famously went to the United States to prey on unsuspecting Americans in a series of basic knowledge questions about Canada. Broadcast throughout Canada, the show *Talking to Americans* tickled many Canadian funny bones, as Americans unknowingly took Mercer's questions to be legitimate. And many of the questions focused on Canada being a frozen tundra.

Ironically, a lot of the naïvete of Americans could be attributed to Canadians themselves, who export comedy oversimplifying Canada's identity as a land mass of ice and snow. It's a strange relationship, in which Canadians enjoy talking up the nastiness of Canadian winters, but then roll their eyes when the Americans take these claims at face value and repeat them as truisms. The story of the hapless American showing up at the border in July with skis attached to the top of his car and seeking directions to the snow fields is a Canadian urban myth that never fails to amuse despite the inability to actually identify such an occurrence.

Mercer, posing as a serious broadcaster for the CBC, parlayed the Canadian identity of a winter haven to comical results. One such exchange broadcast on his special showed him telling Americans the challenges faced by Canada's capital building. Mercer explained to his bemused subjects that this Canadian building was essentially comparable to America's Capitol building, however, it was slightly downscaled and made of ice. Mercer's hope was that by appearing as a legitimate Canadian reporter, and feeding on America's misconceptions about Canada, respondents wouldn't blink an eye at this piece of news. There was much glee among Canadians at what Canadians most enjoy, namely seeing Americans make fools of themselves on our national television. Of course none of this ever makes its way to the American media so the joke loses its ability to humiliate.

Our national capital building — "It's an igloo." Or so Mercer explained to the Americans he talked to on the street. "Canadians are worried about global warming so we are considering putting a dome over it, to preserve our igloo."

The segment showed Americans taking Mercer's microphone and agreeing that the dome would be a splendid idea, and that in building the dome over the ice building, Canadians could create more revenue by making it a tourist destination.

In a major coup, Mercer was even able to get Arkansas Governor Mike Huckabee to appear on camera to say "Congratulations Canada on preserving your national igloo."

Canadians throughout the country laughed at the ways major American politicians could be exposed as being so ignorant about Canadian culture. What Mercer really revealed, however, was exposing how successful Canadians had been in exporting the very image he was exploiting for humorous effect. It's an identity Canadians are very comfortable perpetuating.

American comedians use the same formula as Mercer when they try to appease Canadians when visiting the country. The jokes almost follow the same "paint by number" creation. They cater to the Canadian audience, and allow the visitor to portray themselves as part of Canadian culture, by creating jokes about the winter, followed by jokes about airplane food, and bad drivers. Canadians can't get enough of them.

When popular American late night talk show host Conan O'Brien

Glenbow Alberta Institute, Bill Fitsell Collection NA-2500-4.

Outdoor hockey in Alberta, pre–First World War.

brought his show to Toronto in February 2004, he put to good use this poking of fun at all things Canadian. Hockey, winter coats, and igloos came out in full force. O'Brien's segments were full of winks and nudges to the cold weather, and to hockey, with sketches featuring members of the Toronto Maple Leafs. It made perfect sense.

Conan quickly discovered during his time in Toronto that Tie Domi, at the time arguably the most popular Maple Leafs hockey player, was one of the most significant cultural icons of the city. An unknown figure to anyone south of the border, Domi was an icon that was uniquely Canadian. Like Mr. Bean of Britain, or The Crocodile Hunter in Australia, Domi represented Canada. O'Brien was keen enough to discover that hockey was the defining characteristic of Canadian culture, and leaped at the opportunity of casting Domi in one of his sketches. Not surprisingly, the live Toronto audience lapped it up.

Not only did Conan's live audience laugh, but at times proved these stereotypes true, as audience members would randomly chant "Go Leafs Go" during segments when Conan interviewed proud Canadian Mike Myers. Myers gleefully contrasted the differences between America and Canada, and embraced the crowd.

Despite dozens of stereotypical Canadian characterizations featuring cold weather dwellers, and igloo jokes, the only time Conan's crew caught the ire of Canadians, and in particular Canadian politicians, was when his NBC crew went off the climate script, and did a segment involving a puppet dog poking fun at French culture in Quebec. The furor made its way to Parliament after the segment aired, further illustrating the point that Canadians will laugh, tolerate, and perpetuate jokes about their hockey-loving, cold-weather hoser image, but jokes about the more subtle tensions between Francophones and Anglophones are off limits.

While Canada is a nation made up of both French- and English-speaking Canadians, and has a unique culture, with their ancestors first fighting against one another and then living together, it's not something to be rubbed too sharply or put at the forefront of discussion. It certainly isn't something to be mocked. It's a very delicate relationship, and one upon which politicians are leery about treading. A foreign comedian using a puppet dog to insult the French, put politicians from all sides, French and English, on a hot seat, and created a reaction the O'Brien crew simply could not anticipate. They eventually apologized having learned what humour was tolerated in Canada. In the world of comedy, it's best to stick with something Canadians as a whole accommodate — the Canada identity as a Winter Wonderland. That's funny.

Library and Archives Canada C-14921.

The Queen of the Ice, 1903.

Comedy is not the only place in which the winter climate and Canadian culture meld. It abounds in literature. With poems and stories detailing Canadian winters, the country's cold vast landscape is a source of wonderment, and inspiration to writers who travel throughout its length (and width).

It inspired Canadian novelist and poet George Bowering to write: "This is a country of silent wind piling drift snow in Rocky Mountains, trenches of quiet death, lonely desolation."

Bowering is far from being the only writer to note the cold openness of the vast Canadian landscape. Early British settlers wrote about their first experiences coming to Canada and noted with horror how Canada's winters set the country apart from the more forgiving British weather. Writers would lament Canada's frozen, frigid, and inhospitable terrain.

Many failed to foresee that Canada could ever be a developed nation, much less one to which native Brits would flee. There might be lots of open land, but how could it be valuable if it was covered in snow for much of the year? Early accounts of British writers encountering Canada in the late 1700s included their lament that this was a land rendering inhabitants "void of thought" and impairing mental powers. This unforgiving, frigid landscape would drive people to drinking, gambling, and ultimately breaking down. The moral fibre of society would collapse under such conditions. Winter of such ferociousness would destroy humanity.

Cold and winter have been used to inspire other forms of depressing poetry. It has been unrepentant about the general dreadfulness of Canadian winters. Throughout the 1800s and into the 1900s writers produced works reading like horror stories of a barren, cold wasteland.

In 1946, Patrick Anderson wrote a poem about Canada, which he concluded by stating that the country was a nation that had untapped potential — despite the cold. In his concluding line in "Poem on Canada," he makes reference to Canada's unique climate, calling it "A Cold Kingdom."

> America's attic, an empty room
> a something possible, a chance, a dance
> that is not danced. A cold kingdom.

Conversely, the cold and winter has also been used in poetry as a punchline. In 1971, poet Alden Nowlan, may have been ahead of his time, in combining poetic prose with a Canadian climate jab. He created a poem suggesting that the winter of Canada had unparalleled danger, simply because it is a Canadian winter.

Innocently titled "Canadian January Night," Nowlan's poem reads:

> This is a country
> where a man can die
> simply from being
> Caught outside

Likewise, Roch Carrier's famous hockey sweater story incorporates all facets of Canada's winter culture, from both a French and English perspective and the horror of having to wear the uniform of one's

Photograph by Steele and Co., Manitoba Archives N974.

First Peoples curling five, possibly at Washakada Indian School in Elkhorn, circa 1898.

dreaded rival in an unsympathetic public place. Winter shrivels in its impact besides such humiliation.

Perhaps the relationship between Canadians and the winter is best understood by Canadians transplanted from their homeland. It is now common for Canadian entertainers to head to the United States exporting their talents to a larger audience, but intriguingly, it appears that many of these entertainers can't help sharing stories about their Canadian upbringing in interviews. Comedians such as Howie Mandell and Mike Myers are notorious for going off topic in interviews with stories about their Canadian childhoods. Myers's connection with Canada resulted in a movie project based entirely on his love of Canada's national game. Myers's film, *The Love Guru*, centred around the main character helping to turn around the career of a hockey player on his favourite team, the Toronto Maple Leafs. The movie was a critical and commercial bust, but it affirmed the idea that while Myers hasn't lived in Canada for years, his upbringing certainly remains influential in his writing and producing.

It's a sentiment that is echoed by Canadian writer Blanche Howard who remarked:

> To tell you the truth, in California I missed the wildness of the Canadian winter. There is something stirring about a blizzard, something elemental about pitting oneself against driving, stinging snow in below zero temperatures. I often think it accounts for the general peacefulness of the Canadian character, all the aggressive energy has been used up in battling and surviving nature.

On the other hand, Jack Kent Cooke, owner of the expansion Los Angeles Kings, who entered the National Hockey League in the fall of 1967, was convinced that with 2 million ex pat Canadians in California he'd have no problem selling out his games. Full houses, however, proved hard to come by and a puzzled Cooke finally concluded that the 2 million Canucks had moved there because they hated hockey and by extension that memory of the wildness of the Canadian winter.

Humans are bound by their relationship with nature. Canadian culture stems from decades of long, harsh winters, from unrelenting snowfalls, and short summers. It's simply a reaction to the country's geographic location. It's something that has evolved naturally.

While Canadians have adopted the story of theirs being a land of immigrants, the country still has a collective culture defining the nation as a whole, and that collective cultural identifier has been the harsh Canadian winter. It comes up in conversations wherever Canadians travel. It's something synonymous with Canada, like the British and their tea, or the Spanish with salsa.

Despite the threat that winters will become balmier, for now Canadians still have a collective culture binding them together — a common bond of fighting the frigid winter, of making use of the cold elements, and embracing them, and ultimately of becoming identified with them.

THREE

Winter Sports in Canada from Snowshoeing to Cross-Country Skiing

Immorality reigned on the slopes of Ottawa in the winter of 1885 as young ladies tobogganed long into the night in the company of young men. The Reverend Father Whalen of Ottawa's St. Patrick's Church condemned the mingling of the sexes on the hills of the Rideau valley, and darkly referenced stories recently posted by American journalists in the *New York Clipper*, the day's leading sports and entertainment journal, deploring the goings-on at the Montreal winter carnival.

"It was not innocent, as you might imagine," he warned his congregants. "And even skating carnivals lead to unhappy consequences between the sexes."

Winter was a lively and potentially dangerous season, but usually for reasons unrelated to the padre's *cri de coeur*. For instance, Beverly Ingersoll of Woodstock was so badly injured tobogganing on February 19 of that year that he died on the twenty-fourth. Miss Keachie of Brantford had an elbow dislocated and an arm bruised from an upset on the twenty-first. John Moberly of Collingwood died almost instantly after his toboggan struck a stump on the night of the twenty-sixth.

Later generations, content to while away a winter's evening in the comfort of Internet chat rooms, and a five-hundred-channel television universe, and for whom their snow is cleared from the front driveway by the kid up the street, and who curse the long commute on Monday morning roads slowed by snow-removal vehicles and sludge thrown up on windshields, might wonder at a world in which Canadians confronted winter as something to be enjoyed despite its potential for unsavoury conduct and even death.

On the other hand, Canadians have never really lost that willingness to confront winter as a joyful experience rather than an annoyance. How else can one explain the willingness of parents to endure 5:00 a.m. hockey practices for young Jessica or Ryan? Surely it must be more than a bracing mug of Tim Hortons coffee, though its status as Canada's national stimulant is without rival. Or how does one explain a willingness to drive hundreds of miles from home on dodgy roads for the pleasures of downhill skiing? And we might include the Canada-wide fascination with curling bonspiels, and the ensuing fraternizing between men and women, aided by the possible consumption of popular alcoholic beverages. What would the priest have to say about this?

Canadians have bought the pleasures of indoor, climate-controlled activity and adopted skin-tight lycra outfits to negate winter's worst blasts and look good in the process. They have imposed multiple health and safety rules to lower the risk of on-site calamity, but ultimately they accept their destiny as denizens of a winterized country.

And yet that hasn't stopped them from complaining.

Returning to the winter of 1885, the annual competition for the Ontario Tankard ended in Toronto on February 20. Teams gathered from around the province, having won their regional honours: St. Marys, Scarborough Maple Leafs, Bowmanville, Galt, Hamilton Thistles, Harriston, and Orillia. The latter drew the bye while St. Marys, Hamilton, and Scarborough eliminated their rivals. The next morning Orillia defeated St. Marys as Hamilton did likewise with Scarborough. In the afternoon Orillia won the Tankard, defeating Hamilton by eight points.

According to reports of the day, matches were also held during that time in London, Owen Sound, Thorold, Cobourg, Kincardine, and Listowel.

"*The Grand Trunk Snow Shoe Races: The Last Hurdle*" from the
Canadian Illustrated News, *February 25, 1871.*

Meanwhile in Montreal, revelers were storming the ice palace at that city's annual carnival while upwards of twenty thousand spectators watched. The structure was lit from within and outside while those in command of the fort in their blue blanket coats taunted their white- and red-coated besiegers arrayed in the surrounding square. The latter's attempt to take the fort was declared a failure after a two-hour limit was reached.

Elsewhere, the beginnings of more formal figure-skating competition were on view at Montreal's Victoria Rink. Louis Rubinstein outperformed his rivals in a series of figures including plain forward skating, cross rolls, plain eights, grape-vine, scissors, spins, rocking turns, pivot figures, and locomotive slips. Rubinstein would eventually win international honours in Russia before fleeing that country when it was hinted that they might turn their attention to the visiting Canadian as part of their increasingly ruthless persecution of their own Jewish population. Rubinstein was a major figure in Canadian sports for years, afterwards assuming a prominent leadership role in cycling's Canadian Wheelman's Association

As well, early forms of speed skating were on view at Montreal's Crystal Rink where the victor covered five miles in twenty minutes and forty-three seconds, while at a masquerade carnival in Saint John, New Brunswick, John Gilchrist won a three-mile race.

The toboggan experience was likewise the precursor of a number of modern sporting pursuits from bobsledding to luge and skeleton. The *New York Clipper* in 1885 dramatically described the sensation:

> The sharp edges of the straining board cut rainbows of snow spray that hiss at you and cover your beard with chilly diamonds and Angelina's hair with priceless jewels; from either side the grinding crystals fly behind you like sparks from a grindstone. You have hardly swallowed your heart again when you are at the foot of the slope, and, with the bound of a shark touched with the steel, the sled, striking the level, springs a dozen feet into the air, and landing on the level snow crust, speeds onward, with scarcely lessening speed, till it stops more than a mile away from the hill where you started.

Snowshoeing, "The Favourite Pastime This Winter" from the Canadian Illustrated News, *January 21, 1871.*

Notable about all of these extensive accounts from the *New York Clipper* is that there is no mention of hockey. Simple forms of the game were played at this time, having been a popular folk custom throughout the century, but it had still not broken through to an organized tipping point from which the popular media would deem it worthy of reporting.

As popular as all of these other sports were, however, they all took second place to the robust Canadian delight with snowshoeing. Snowshoeing is so very Canadian-specific. Developed by First Nations in response to the peculiar conditions of a northern climate, it arrived in primitive form with the first Eurasian nomads ten thousand years ago, sometime after the last ice age had withdrawn.

Long ago, before recorded history, travelling on snow in the northern reaches of Asia had bequeathed two approaches — one had depended on long, angular pieces of wood suitable for more variable topography, while the other, on flatter surfaces, was an amalgam of catgut and wooden frame for a plodding, but necessarily deliberate movement.

It's likely that both types of primitive winter footwear immigrated along with their Asian creators as they moved west and east, but only one of the two survived in the new lands in which they eventually settled. In northern Europe the long, angular pieces of wood evolved into skiing in its downhill and cross-country forms.

The other geographically appropriate, and wider-bottomed tennis racket–like shoe, proved more adaptable to the American continent, though not amongst those who settled in the most northern territory. Inuit lacked the necessary raw material of wood, while a frozen tundra of wind-packed snow or sea ice presented conditions similar to a concrete sidewalk, thus making unnecessary the use of what became the snowshoe.

Athapascans in the west and Algonquin in the east, the descendants of those who settled south (in relative terms) of their Arctic cousins, were the North American innovators in developing what eventually became hundreds of variants of a bear-paw design suitable for different regional conditions. A longer and narrower streamlined tool for "skating" through woodland regimes, in which snow lay packed and less evenly distributed owing to trees and other encumbrances, met the needs of hunters. For open fields in which snow lay untamed and porous, a shorter bear-paw model was preferred. Skiing, on the other hand, was not successfully introduced into Canada until the late nineteenth century by northern European immigrants from Scandinavia and Germany.

The French were the first European adventurers to settle in today's Canada. They soon recognized the snowshoe's value for both the fur trade and their military security. The English had superiority in manpower, firepower, and European technology, but because they were based farther south on the continent, in what is essentially today's United States, they had less need for this unconventional footwear. Thus the men of New France, with their snowshoe prowess, were often able to surprise and overwhelm many technically superior English garrisons.

The two (as there were two skirmishes given the same name) Battle on Snowshoes near Lake George in 1757 and 1758 confirmed for the British the military value of the snowshoe. In the first battle the French lacked snowshoes and so struggled in snow up to their knees, while in the second the outnumbered British were able to fight longer than anticipated because they wore snowshoes while marching through more than a metre of snow.

In a few years the British had driven the French from North America. But any superiority snowshoe footwear provided was obviously irrelevant a few years later as American colonists tossed the British out of today's United States.

The lowly but effective snowshoe might have faded from prominence, or at least remained solely the everyday resource for First Nations outside of mainstream observation, had it not obtained a new and very different life in the next century. By this time the English, having lost their brief hegemony in North America, had to figure out what to do with a Canadian colony that the French philosopher Voltaire had once derisively described as a few acres of snow.

It provided an opportunity for snowshoeing's third coming following its long First Nations evolution and its more recent adoption by Francophone fur traders.

By the nineteenth century, Anglophone Canadians had begun to slowly realize that the business of survival no longer required their complete attention. An emerging middle class of business, bureaucratic, and academic types was discovering the modern concept of leisure.

Manitoba Archives, Foote Collection N2175.

An unidentified group of snowshoers, circa 1914.

In 1882 Hugh Wylie Becket wrote *The Montreal Snow Shoe Club: Its History and Record with a Synopsis of Racing Events of Other Clubs Through the Dominion from 1840 to the Present Times*, tracing his club's origins from that year when twelve friends gathered for country tramps every Saturday afternoon. Where did the inspiration come from? Perhaps it was nothing more than the imaginative perspective of one intrepid participant who wanted to get out with his buddies for the day.

Within three years the friends, having gathered such a large body of fellow "trampers," concluded that a more formal organization was needed. They elected their first club president, Colonel Charles Ermatinger, a one-time partner in the North West Company. In so doing they had perhaps unwittingly established one of the first sporting clubs in North America. It was an organization with no direct utilitarian purpose, but one based on the somewhat dormant, but always resilient, sporting heritage of humanity, and the fond wish of men and women for good fellowship in each other's company.

The Montreal Snow Shoe Club grew in popularity, flourishing for the better part of the nineteenth century. Races were first held in 1843 on a 6.5-kilometre course at the St. Pierre Racetrack. Deroche, a Metis nor'wester, affixed spikes to his shoes to counter the challenges of ice-covered ground. He outlasted Nicholas Hughes, a clerk to the garrison quartermaster. Hugh Becket described the five Natives who followed as "rather disgusted with the advance civilization had made."

Nicholas Hughes and Edouard Lamontagne were the premier snowshoers of the day, at least among non-Native participants. Neither corresponded to the elitist makeup of most club members.

The sporting world of that era was an ongoing struggle between two types of competitors. On the one hand were those for whom sports was an outlet for their social position, a chance to network with their social and workplace equals, and a place to extol the virtues of their privileged education. Ultimately, for them it, was a manly Christian demonstration of superior physical and mental capacity. Sports were a blessed retreat from the purposefulness of income and status, and participants had no expectation, or desire, for financial reward. Eventually they became proponents of the cult of the amateur.

On the other hand were those for whom sports, while pleasurable and a demonstration of superior skill, also had the potential to be a profession. Sports was increasingly a utilitarian realm in which skilled competitors strived not just for victory, but financial gain. They were deemed to be professionals. In most cases this was directly connected to their position in life.

The necessary skills for the sport in which they engaged perfectly met their peculiar talent, and often their job, outside the sporting realm. Men who worked on Toronto's waterfront in this era for instance, whether ferrying taxis across the lake or undertaking related physical work, were, by the era's definition, incapable of being amateur rowers, regardless of whether they were rewarded for their sports participation. They were considered to have a sporting advantage because of their employment.

Author's collection.

"*A Snow Tramp in High Park, Toronto, Canada.*"

Hughes's plebian employment made him an outsider among Snow Shoe Club members, and Lamontagne, as a French Canadian in an Anglophone organization, was also an anomaly. But it would be unwise to assume they were not welcomed or supported. Club members, for instance, adopted colourful uniforms, brightly coloured sashes, and the *Tuque Bleue*, thus paying homage to the French Canadian habitant blue woollen headgear, originally introduced into Canada by the Normandy French.

One might conclude that the dominant Anglo culture was merely adopting aspects of a submissive French culture while denying them access to real power. The experience of American whites in usurping certain elements of black culture, while creating a segregated separateness in the century following the American Civil War, supports this theory. On the other hand such cultural exchanges may also be the earliest, and possibly only, means by which two cultures can begin a process of managing not just the process of living together, but of undoing their unequal standing.

Nicholas Hughes was a hero and leader of the club for many years. In time he earned the sobriquet "Evergreen," and when he died in 1884, club members organized a snowshoe tramp to his grave in Côte-des-Neiges cemetery on Veterans Night. It was a tradition that lasted into the 1930s.

Snowshoe races were common by the 1850s. Professionals and amateurs often competed alongside each other. A First Nations hero, Ignace won an 1850 race over 9.6 kilometres in a time of under fifty minutes. In 1856 he finished a 6.5-kilometre race in just over thirty minutes. Sir George Simpson was so impressed that he selected Ignace to accompany his final expedition searching for the remains of the Arctic explorer Sir John Franklin and his crew.

(As an aside, Franklin's lost crew may have played an early primitive form of ice hockey in the Canadian North. Recent research indicates that men under John Franklin's command both skated and played a game recognizable as early hockey on a small lake beside Great Bear Lake on October 25, 1825. Questions remain, however, as to whether they skated while playing this early form of hockey, or whether these activities were undertaken separately at different times during the day. Even had they been playing an early game of hockey on skates it's incorrect to say that this location is the birthplace for hockey, since the game had no impact on the later evolution of the sport. It is a curious and possibly early experiment notable for its imaginative quality rather than being a trend setting innovation.)

As the skill of snowshoe competitors improved, however, so did the prize money, whether under the table or in full view.

A hardy amateur from the favoured social elite bemoaned the loss of fun, decrying, "The hope still lingers fondly with some of us that those days may return when we can leave our office stools to compete with some chance of success instead of resorting to the laborious systems of training which now threatens to bring our gentlemanly sports to the level of professionalism."

The robust character of the sport reached a point from which Native craftsmen producing lightweight shoes refused to sell to non-Natives. A Native designer, Narcisse, introduced a 680-gram shoe in 1844, a decided advantage over the 1.8-kilogram model most European descended racers used. The weight of Native footwear continued this downward trend so that by 1871 it had dropped to below 450 grams. In confronting the challenge of

Manitoba Archives, Foote Collection N7408.

Canadian Pacific Railway's Ladies' Snowshoe Club, February 9, 1922.

modern technology, mainstream European-descended organizers passed a rule prohibiting the use in racing of shoes weighing less than 680 grams. As well, a minimum width of 25.5 centimetres was also mandated.

Such rules, while seemingly fair on the surface, eroded the spirit of imagination on which sports progress, and any sport that freezes itself in a particular innovative straitjacket, eventually ensures its decline and fall. Such would be the fate of snowshoeing, though its momentum ensured many years of success ahead.

While sporting competition may have attracted the majority of popular attention, it was the recreational aspect that garnered the greatest participation. It was a fascination that confronted those delicate nineteenth-century boundaries between men and women and provided at least a temporary public meeting place.

Lord Dufferin in his 1873 address to Montreal's snowshoers called it:

> A subject of gratitude that ladies should engage on equal
> terms with gentlemen in several of these sports, and

even occasionally surpass them...When the people of a country could not only bear up against the rigour of an Arctic winter, but ... make it serve to exhibit their grace and charms, they offered a beautiful example, and assisted in no inconsiderable measure to make the men brave, manly and martial.

There are few more prosaic accounts of this era's conviviality on snow than the records of the Montreal Snow Shoe Club. Hugh Becket described an 1871 hike of the club to Lachine:

The club mustering 26 men met upon the Lacrosse ground for a tramp to Lachine. The day was bright and clear, in fact everything that the most fastidious snowshoer could have desired ... All care was thrown to the winds that whistled cheerily through the trees, "sweet freedom's happy notes we love to hear," as trudging along, taking fences and rails with a bound, and a hearty laugh as a novice, attempting to follow in the footsteps of some veteran "hurdler" found himself buried to his waist belt in the snow. Soon we "struck" the "switch" and a rousing "tally ho" from our leader was the signal for a grand dash, and the honour of "first man in" ... After supper ... the dance — which is well calculated to settle (or rather unsettle some might say) the most indigestible of meals — was indulged in till about 9:45, when the "Home" signal was given, "God Save the Queen" sung, three cheers for that same noble lady, the trails struck and after an hour and a half's traveling the city reached.

And no doubt they enjoyed some of the multitude of snowshoe songs, sung to the popular tunes of the day. The latter circulated in the days before radio and phonograph by means of the travelling entertainer, sheet music, and the memories of those able to travel.

Peter Georgen, town druggist in Barrie, with his snowshoes.

Stephen Foster's "Camptown Races," while notably "chart-topping" and sadly racist, nevertheless spawned many adaptations. The Montreal Club was no exception, penning "The Snow Shoe Races," a tune that most people could sing to this day to Foster's air.

Canadian fellows, sing this song
Hurrah! Hurrah!
Wish the winter was nine months long
Hurrah! Hurrah! Hurrah!
Toboggan, sleigh and slim snow shoe
Hurrah! hurrah!
Wish we had nothing else to do
Hurrah! Hurrah! Hurrah!

Chorus — Away! In Indian fyle [sic]
We tramp for many a mile
We shout hurrah! For the manly race
And welcome the maiden's smile.

Saturday afternoons at two
Fellows with toques of red and blue
Muster on the snow shoe ground
The quarter track to travel round.

At the word they toe the mark
Runners pale and Indians dark
Pistol cracks, they're off like a shot,
Weather cold, but the race gets hot.

Eight more verses follow, with the ending as follows:

Canada wants plucky men,
Able with arm, as well as pen
In the tramping on snow shoe
There's the national work we do.

Dinners, songs, and woodland tramps characterized the lively affairs of the Montreal snowshoers, but they were not without awareness of encroaching rivals. In a "Toast to Our Winter Sports," proposed by the chairman, drunk with Highland honours, and followed by the popular song, "Tramp, tramp on snow shoes tramping," Mr. R.D. McGibbon sounded a faint warning in 1881:

> I have said that snowshoeing is the chief of our winter sports, but it is by no means the only one. Who can describe the pleasures of tobogganing, whether enjoyed by the rustic school boy on his primitive imitation made of two or three staves of a barrel fastened together, or practiced by the wealthy on their cushioned toboggans made of birch, upon a carefully kept hill! The feeling experienced in descending a cote, bounding over the unyielding snow, at lightening speed is indescribable, and when to the pleasures of the sport itself there is added the not infrequent presence of the fair sex, it would baffle the temerity of the boldest to attempt a word picture of the sensation.
>
> Skating too, though not a peculiarly Canadian sport, is enjoyed here as nowhere else, and the phrase which Lord Dufferin applied to it on a certain memorable occasion is admittedly apposite. He said it was the true "poetry of motion" of which professors of aesthetics speak – and it is.
>
> Then again we have curling, hockey on ice, shinty on skates. They too need no praise or mention.
>
> And I must conclude without referring as I might, to the delicious sensation of a drive, perchance by the side of the girl you love, in well-robed sleigh — drawn by a fleet horse — upon good roads — by moonlight such as the Canadians alone enjoy.
>
> I have said enough — very imperfectly I regret — to convince you if indeed you need conviction, that

our winter season is one that has the most pleasurable accompaniments, and that our winter sports are not only enjoyable in themselves, but thoroughly appreciated by us Canadians.

Montrealers were not content to celebrate their sports only in their original settings. With the great movement of settlers into western Canada in the late nineteenth century, it was only natural they took their sports with them. In 1878 a club composed chiefly of old Montrealers was formed in Winnipeg. In February 1879 they held their first races.

In gradual measure Canadians were defining their country through their love of winter sports and their embrace of the season.

Snowshoeing had never been more popular, but its future was, unbeknownst to its supporters, under threat.

Many reasons are given for a sport's decline. For one, new games often suddenly rise in popularity. By the late nineteenth century, a serious interloper, "hockey on ice, or shinty on skates," was raising its head as a challenger for Canadian enthusiasm. Lacrosse was one of the first to fall from favour. That game's increasing violence has often been cited, but that flies in the face of its popular replacement by hockey, a game if anything, more dangerous, and in which fighting is condoned as virtually a part of the sport's culture and identity. No other game is quite so open in tolerating such a perversion of its own play.

Snowshoeing's decline around this time may owe at least something to its staid character in contrast to hockey's robust unpredictability. By the time of the First World War, many snowshoe organizers had switched over to that sport. Likewise, Montreal's leadership in winter carnivals, begun in the 1870s by intrepid snowshoers, had gradually given way to Quebec City's more aggressive promotion. Many Montrealers had taken up the new sport of skiing.

As early as 1879 the *Canadian Illustrated News* had depicted the Norwegians of Montreal participating on what the magazine called Norwegian snowshoes. Those "snowshoes" were in fact a primitive form of cross-country ski. Recalling the evolution of the two methods of travel on snow — the snowshoe type in North America, and the narrower ski

Simcoe County Archives.

The Booth family in Barrie, Ontario.

type in northern Europe — it was only a matter of time before the two, originally developed in Asia, would meet again.

Fridtjof Nansen's ski trek across Greenland in 1888 helped popularize skiing, at least in Europe. The sport of downhill and slalom skiing slowly emerged. Not surprisingly, the more dramatic potential of skiing, particularly as it transformed beyond its cross-country form to the thrill of the downhill, made snowshoeing look somewhat antiquated and dowdy in comparison.

Later in his life the seemingly immortal Herman "Jackrabbit" Smith-Johannsen (1875–1987) noted the way his trapper guides through the Ontario bush in 1902 had worn snowshoes, but that twenty years later they were travelling on skis, using snowshoes only where conditions dictated.

Snowshoe organizers and their descendants saw nothing unusual in adapting the organizational model of snowshoeing to the spirited world of skiing and by 1905 social ski tours had become popular.

It awaited only the development of improved technology for skis and chairlifts, and the introduction of specialized resorts to complete the transformation.

FOUR

Canadian Winter Sports from Curling to Snowboarding

The father and grandfather of this book's authors told an unnerving story meant to warn us against, we suppose, similar folly. Having fought through North Africa and into Italy with the British Army in the Second World War, he was part of the occupation force in Austria at the war's conclusion. One might have thought there was enough terror in those years to last a lifetime but then he joined some comrades in that postwar period on an Austrian bobsled run.

It was, he told us, the most frightening experience of his life.

The sport has an honourable European heritage dating back to the late nineteenth century. Not content with the rush of a toboggan ride down the famous Cresta Run at St. Moritz, the hometown Swiss had added runners and thus unwittingly developed what became the sport of bobsledding. Early enthusiasts were British and American visitors to the site, but it wasn't one of them named "Bob" who gave the sport its name. The nomenclature is more functional. Early users thought that they could increase the speed of the descent by "bobbing," or jerkily moving, their torsos from one side to another. In fact, the additional friction created by exposing themselves to the elements marginally slowed the sled's descent.

Competition began at the Cresta Run in 1898. Five-passenger sleds were mandated and a minimum of two women were part of the complement. Borrowing ideas from an equally new invention, the four runners were situated like the wheels of a car. Toboggans had been both fast and dangerous, but at least there was significant drag on their progress down steep slopes, whereas the bobsled with its main frame off the surface obtained speeds at which even minimal control was impossible. Accidents and death were common.

Finally, a cautious official concluded that a somewhat reduced slope was preferred and so an artificial course with a gentler incline was eventually introduced at St. Moritz in 1902.

It took a little bit of experimentation to sort out the contours of this new design. In recognition of the need to balance the thrill and danger of the sport, however, the average slope was finally settled at an eight-to-fifteen percent lean.

Once the problems had been resolved, bobsledding spread to other Alpine countries. There were up to a hundred runs by the time of the first European championships at the start of the First World War. The *Fédération Internationale de Bobsleigh et de Tobogganing* (FIBT) was established in 1923. With standard rules, the sport was ready for its inclusion in the first Winter Olympics at Chamonix, France, in 1924. In Canada the first artificial bobsled run was built in 1911 at Montebello, Quebec, and by 1964 Canadians had won a gold medal in the four-man event.

More recently, bobsledding followers were enthusiasts of a state-of-the-art run built for the 1988 Winter Olympics in Calgary.

The bobsled formula requires that the run be at minimum 1,500 metres with fifteen or twenty turns, as much to demonstrate that the result isn't simply determined by who gets the fastest start at the top of the run. Significant skill is required to master the split-second possibilities of lost time because of poorly managed adjustment to these turns.

Nevertheless four-man squads often hire former one-hundred-metre dash athletes to help kick-start their run.

Manitoba Archives, Foote Collection 1075.

Lady curlers in the Winnipeg Board of Trade Building, circa 1906.

The bobsled run's preparation resembles what one might think of as a madman's recipe. Wet snow is laid over a concrete or stone foundation. The snow is then soaked with water. Iced sidewalls and banks keep the sleds on the course, though this hasn't kept some from becoming airborne by flying off the run on the straightaway. And while in the four-man competition two riders are essentially passengers once the pushing off from the starting line is complete, they do perform a modest leaning function.

We suspect, however, that they put our father/grandfather in the front seat, where he couldn't just bend down and await the end of the run. The driver of both the two- and four-person sled is, after all, the key rider in getting the maximum speed from the sled by managing hairpin turns of more than 180 degrees, and retaining his nerve at speeds of nearly 160 kilometres an hour.

Other Olympic sports have had similarly unusual starts.

Other than the excitement occasioned by Myriam Bédard's two gold-medal performance in Norway in 1994, biathlon hardly registers on the Canadian consciousness.

The sport's combination of cross-country skiing along with target shooting is one of those events that begs the question by the outsider as to what other combinations of apparently unrelated skills are possible to create a new winter sport. The biathlete skis with a rifle over a prescribed distance to the shooting range where the competitor takes five shots at five targets at a distance of fifty metres from a prone position. A time penalty or additional laps are assessed for missed shots. The racer then skis another loop, and comes back to the shooting range for another set of shots from a standing position.

The origins of biathlon grew from the two linked activities of hunting and winter warfare. Scandinavian bow-and-arrow hunters, for instance, travelled on primitive skis long after the Roman poet Virgil described a hunting expedition on skis in 400 BC. And just as later military commanders in the early twentieth century adopted the bicycle with a rifle strapped to its side in the cause of warfare, so too did generals of the sixteenth century refine the idea of skiing regiments. In both cases, one winces at this translation of harmless recreation into such militaristic ends.

Organized competition dates at least to the eighteenth century in Norway, the country which, to this day, is the Winter Olympics supreme medal winner.

Years later, a military ski patrol race based on the elements of the sport was held at the first Winter Olympics in 1924. Its demonstration nature continued until after the Second World War, perhaps because organizers were never sure that such a utilitarian exercise could have sporting legitimacy.

What was known as the patrol race became the biathlon by the mid 1950s. The sport's first world championship was held in Austria in 1958. Twenty-five athletes from seven countries started the first twenty-kilometre race.

Cardboard targets such as those found in police training shooting ranges were used at first, but they were later replaced by glass discs. Large, army-rifle calibres were replaced by small-bore (.22) rifles in the late 1970s, and women's competition was added for the 1992 Winter Olympics.

The Toronto Curling Club (The Red Jacket Rink) — the Caledonian match on the Don River, 1870, though another source suggests it may be from 1872 on Toronto Bay.

The sport had evolved from an obscure sidelight to a mildly popular television event, one legitimized by its place in the Olympic menu.

Ski jumping on the other hand is, perhaps along with penny-farthing cycling, a sport the average person watches with the bemused knowledge that not only is this something they could never, or would never do, but is a performance aided by trick photography, or in today's age, computer manipulation.

The opening passage of a famous ABC television *Wide World of Sports* show announced that they were spanning the globe to bring viewers "the constant variety of sport … the thrill of victory … and the agony of defeat … the human drama of athletic competition."

The opening sequence had several memorable moments over the decades, but ski jumper Vinko Bogatai was its unhappy face. In 1970 his failed mis-jump and amazing crash at the end of the ramp before ever taking off, was featured for the rest of the decade along with the words "… and the agony of defeat." He and his sport symbolized the hard-luck nature of athletic competition.

The sport of ski jumping, in less haunting circumstances than these, dates back to at least 1860 when Norway's Sondre Norheim jumped thirty metres without poles over a rock in a Scandinavian version of the popular North American fascination with barrel jumping. Not surprisingly, few were prepared to challenge the apparent madness of flying unprotected through the air. Norheim's bizarre feat, and his record, had there been a Guinness Book of World Records, held for over three decades.

By the start of the twentieth century, however, the madness had given way to curiosity and then to cautious experimentation. New records were set as other intrepid daredevils, in the spirit of those challenging the flat earth theory, or less dauntingly the four-minute mile, took up Norheim's challenge.

Gradually the sport developed its own specialist technique with an aerodynamic approach called the Kongsberger, developed by Thulin Thams, a first Olympic champion in 1924. The jumper's upper body was bent at the hips as he or she leaned forward with arms extended at the front. Suddenly, adventurous athletes were leaping more than one hundred metres. By the mid-1950s, a Swiss jumper named Andreas Daescher had further refined the technique by holding his arms backwards, close to the body, while maintaining a more extreme forward lean. In 1985 a Swedish jumper, Jan Bokloev, spread the tips of his skis into a "V" shape, causing laughter among rivals and penalties from the judges. His victories quickly lead all jumpers to adopt the "V"-style.

The sport continues to amaze and mystify viewers as to the improbability of its exercise. Having stood at the top of such a course in Trondheim, Norway, in 2000, one of this book's authors remains amazed at its practice.

The next sports are best appreciated by briefly turning back to Fred Grant for his memories of the hill and toboggan in Barrie, a sport that is today advanced in technology, but still retains the adventure of its long-ago ancestor:

Author's collection.

"Canadian Winter Sports: Skating on the Don River, Toronto, Canada."

The good old pastime of coasting should not be forgotten. Barrie used to possess some dandy coasting hills, and I presume they are still there, though perhaps not as generally used for bobsledding as in olden days. It was generally agreed at the time that the "bobs" owned and piloted by myself and those belonging to Billy Moore and Ed Greenwood were the best in town, and many an interesting race was held in which the results were about fifty-fifty.

Old Richard Whitebread, who had a carpenter shop in the east end, always made out sleighs and fashioned the long, connecting elm boards that would bend but would not break under any load, and he took about as much interest in having them just so-so as we ourselves did. Any number from ten to fourteen or sixteen could be crowded on … and though this is strictly confidential, the girls didn't object to being crowded up tight when coasting. Of course when there were bumps in the hill or something that prevented smooth going, there weren't always as many passengers at the end of the ride as there were at the beginning, for someone was certain to be joggled off.

Creswicke's Hill had a dangerous turn in it, as did also Bosanko's Hill, and which we overcame to some extent by "banking" the turn with snow and then poring on water to freeze it solid.

Toboggans have a long and respected history, but their identification with childhood perhaps lessens the adult seriousness of their use. Two toboggan-like Olympic events, however, have gained Olympic legitimacy: the luge and skeleton. They reflect the value of a name change.

The skeleton is the heavier of the two weighing in at nearly forty-five kilograms for a single person sled as opposed to just over twenty kilograms for the single-person luge.

Lugers go down feet first, steering by means of legs and shoulders, but while in the skeleton, the slider's head leads out and steers by use of his or her feet.

Luge at the Winter Olympics dates back to 1964, while skeleton had an older, and sporadic Olympic history before returning to the program in 2002 for both men and women.

Everyone who has gone downhill on a sled figures they could participate in this event and they could, but like our father/grandfather, they would regret the choice after just one descent.

Snowboarding, on the other hand, appears to have less dangerous potential. It is part of a family, including surfing and skateboarding, associated with the counterculture movement of the 1960s — laid-back, and perhaps not quite serious in its intentions. Those two sports are often seen as the main influence behind snowboarding for the seamless way those enthusiasms were blended together on winter slopes, probably sometime in the 1950s. The winter sport, however, was noted for its "extreme" nature and was thus placed outside mainstream competition.

Snowboarding gained greater legitimacy throughout the 1960s. A long period of experimentation included novel features such as a rope attached on the front tip of the board and steel tacks to hold the rider's

Library and Archives Canada C-18653.

The Dawson Curling Club Bonspiel in Dawson, Yukon Territory.

feet in place. The renegade character of snowboarders and the evolving and still unfinished nature of their equipment evolution often led to their being ostracized from mainstream ski resorts, and so they discovered and developed their own slopes.

Design, materials, and techniques gradually improved through the seventies and eighties. In the fifteen-year period from 1983 to 1998, the sport went from acceptance in fewer than 10 percent of the established ski areas to general approval in virtually all such places. It first appeared as an Olympic sport in Nagano in 1998. Almost immediately, its "outsider" reputation reared its head as Canada's Ross Rebagliati was at first stripped of his gold medal when traces of marijuana were found in his system. He was eventually reinstated, continued in the sport, and went on to have a successful career as a consultant and commentator on the *Outdoor Life Network*.

Skiing participation has declined alongside snowboarding's continuing growth to over 3.4 million participants. Predictions suggest snowboarding will pass downhill skiing participation by 2015.

Another alternative sport sensation, freestyle skiing, combines the skill of skiing with the acrobatic flourish of aerial twists. In the late 1960s and 1970s the sport's turns and flips were referred to somewhat derisively as "hot-dogging." Danger, an absence of strict rules, and lack of a strong, central organization ensured its anarchic free-spirit character dominated public perception.

Despite its spate of injuries, the sport was recognized in 1979 by the International Ski Federation. A Freestyle World Cup circuit was gradually popularized, allowing the sport to move beyond its carefree days. Introduced as a demonstration event at the Calgary Winter Olympics in 1988, its mogul-skiing form became part of the Albertville Games in 1992, while aerials were added in 1994 to the Lillehammer Games.

Short-track speed skating, on the other hand, is one of those sports spectators could imagine children innocently inventing on a nearby frozen pond.

They would set up some boundary markers. Kids would then strap on their skates and race around the circuit until either only one of them was left standing, or the required laps had been completed.

Its spirit was captured by our old friend Fred Grant:

> The Mary Street skating rink opened about 1876. By that time, as the old wooden-based rockers and heel-screw skates had been replaced with the spring "Acme" and the clamp "Climax," you had got a pair of nickeled ones at Christmas, which were the envy of the other boys. "She" had also learned to skate, and was now such a graceful fairy on the ice you eagerly sought permission as her escort for each band number.
>
> The memories of those early boyhood skating seasons are happy ones, for, boys and girls, you were all carefree together, and it was a joy just to be alive. But some other boy also wanted her for the next "band" and as they skated off together you consoled yourself as you joined the rest of your cronies in a spirited game of cross-tag, "crack-the-whip," or "pull-away," in the

Curling on the St. Lawrence River opposite Montreal, 1878.

course of which many a spill was occasioned to the older skaters, when some whizzing, dodging boy would attempt to go through any opening as wide as a lath that offered escape; even between partners.

Official accounts suggest that short-track speed skating was developed in the early twentieth century in North America and after the First World War attracted interest in Great Britain, Japan, France, Belgium, and Australia. Its legitimacy was confirmed by the International Skating Union (ISU) in 1967, and official competitions began in 1976. By 1988 it was a demonstration event at the Calgary Olympic Winter Games, eventually reaching medal status at the 1992 Albertville Winter Games.

The sport takes place on a 111.12-metre oval track within a standard hockey rink. It is distinguished by tight corners with the athlete bracing themselves in the turn by extending a hand to the ice much like motorcycle racers. However, unlike many winter sports that determine a winner by either a judging point system or a race against the clock, short-track speed skaters compete against each other.

While contact is not part of the sport, it only takes the accidental fall of one racer to bring down the rest of the field. This is part of both the charm, but also the unpredictability of the sport.

At the 2002 Winter Olympics, Australian Steven Bradbury won the men's one-thousand-metre race and was dubbed the "Accidental Hero" after all four of the other skaters in the final, including the American Apolo Anton Ohno and South Korea's Ahn Hyun-Soo fell in the last turn of the race. Bradbury was the last man on the track and too far behind to be brought down. As a result he became Australia's first-ever Winter Olympics gold medalist.

The short-track relay in which four skaters take turns tagging their teammate as part of the circuit changes can be even wilder, with so many athletes on the ice surface at any one time.

Far more sedate is another recent addition to the Winter Olympics. Curling has provided Canadians with an almost arrogant self-belief that their men and women should never lose. For while this game has its roots in a somewhat ancient Scottish tradition, its best players are often those representing competing Canadian provinces rather than those of other nations.

In Scottish lore, references to the game reach back into the seventeenth century and its play no doubt goes even further back, but our knowledge is limited by the lack of adequate reporting. By the eighteenth century it was celebrated in the poetry of Robbie Burns as he wrote in "Tam Samson's Elegy":

> When Winter muffles up his cloak
> And binds the mire like a rock,
> Then to the loch the Curlers flock
> Wi' gleesome speed.

Of course conditions could ruin many a Scottish winter, a hazard less likely to befall enthusiasts in Canada. Clubs had already been organized in Montreal by the early nineteenth century, making them some of the earliest such sporting organizations in the country. At first haggis and whiskey dominated post-competition celebration, but gradually as the sport spread beyond its initial Scottish cohort, so did the menu.

In Ontario, Dr. Adam Ford recalled his early curling encounters:

Manitoba Archives N811.

The Anna Gibson School speed skating team, circa 1933.

My first experience in curling was on the river Thames at Woodstock in 1848 and the peculiarity of the game makes me feel like making a record of it. Scottish settlers had settled in Zorra Township and had evidently played the game somewhere up in that township … The ice had been laid out with tees about thirty yards apart, and stepped off. There were only two rings — the "potlid" and the outer ring which enclosed the "House." The stones were flat boulders picked up in the fields, weighing about, I should say, fifteen to twenty pounds each, with no handles, the players bringing their stones in bags. The stones were pitched along the ice as a ten-pin player tosses his ball along the alley. There was a hog-score: the brooms were sticks over two feet long with blue beech twigs tied round the end and the sweeping was whipping the ice in front of the stones.

Adam Ford is one of the more noted figures in nineteenth-century Canadian sport. He witnessed what is likely the first baseball game in Ontario in 1838, which he wrote about many years later, having fled to Colorado after he had been arrested at horse-racing's Queen's Plate on charges of poisoning a Temperance advocate.

Granite stones were common in Scotland and it was from these that the Scottish game took its name of the "channel-stane." Their restricted supply in Canada, however, meant Canadians often resorted to stones made of maple or beech with iron handles to allow for gripping. Gradually, bell-shaped irons replaced these at least in Quebec, where wood often stuck to the ice in mild conditions, while granite cracked in the cold. An annual bonspiel, a word derived from the Danish *bondespil*, meaning "a rustic game," was soon the most highly anticipated event of the winter season as teams gathered from around the province.

The rustic game's appellation also gave way to the more robust description of "the roaring game" as players shouted commands to each other and brooms cleared snow and dirt from the path. Players soon learned, however, that this sweeping slightly changed the condition of the ice, causing the stone to move in ways conducive to the strategic interests of one or the other team.

By 1876 the game had reached Manitoba and the Scottish custom of playing for a barrel of oatmeal to be distributed to the poor was continued with the contents provided to the city's hospital. Soon not only Manitobans, but those in present-day Saskatchewan and Alberta would be among the sport's premier players, the result of a much longer winter season.

In the East, open-air bonspiels, like one of the last held in Burlington Bay outside Hamilton in 1875, gradually gave way to the sport's move indoors, a function of both more predictable ice conditions and an attempt to counter the fierceness of snow and wind. Nevertheless, these early barn-like structures merely provided a closed venue for what was still natural ice. In some ways they resembled modern ice-fishing huts, though at least the latter might have some heating provided by a generator. The early curling barns would await the arrival of artificial ice-making processes before they truly left the rough-and-tumble world of the outside elements.

In a spirit of camaraderie, and to the air of "Willie Brewed a Peck

Saskatchewan Archives Bureau R-A 4531.

Outdoor curling in Prince Albert, Saskatchewan, circa 1900–05.

o' Maut," curlers, like snowshoers of an earlier generation, continued to sing well into the twentieth century, odes such as that below:

> Now, brothers in the roaring game,
> Come, join a curling stave with me,
> as if your soul were in the stane,
> and heaven itself were near the tee.
> The soop, soop, soop! Soop, soop, soop!
> And draw the creepin' stane a wee;
> the ice may thaw, the day may snaw,
> but aye we're merry round the tee.

Curling is now firmly placed in the roster of Winter Olympic events, but this doesn't mean there will be no new ones. In the spirit of that quest, a few ideas are suggested for the consideration of organizers.

One such candidate is barrel jumping. It's a simple sport and one that Canadians dominate. For many years it was featured on American general sports television broadcasts because of its novelty. The baseball great Jackie Robinson actually judged one such contest in upper New York State in the early 1950s.

Skaters, like those in track and field's long jump, approach a row of barrels at the greatest speed possible and attempt to clear whatever number are placed in their way. Only distance matters so one can adopt any style that gets the job done.

Skate jumping has a long history with the Dutch, incorporating local impediments like fences, gates, and walls in the path of long distance skaters. Use of the barrel, however, is credited to a former speed-skating champion Irving Jaffee. While it does have a carnival character, part of its appeal is also the self control, speed, and bravery of competitors — not too different from skateboarding and hot-dog skiing.

Participants build up speed by circling the rink several times before attacking a series of barrels lined up width ways side by side. Solid steel drums would be too risky and dangerous, so organizers now rely on look-alike products made of fibreboard or even cardboard. As such, the barrels provide a softer landing for those who fail to clear them. Those who make it over all the barrels have a harder time as they land directly on the ice. No one has found a way to cushion that encounter!

The competition starts at twelve barrels, but it can reach eighteen or more. Canadians, particularly those from Quebec, have dominated the sport.

Ice biking is another pursuit with Winter Olympic possibilities.

An Australian, Daavid Turnbull (yes there is a double "a"), was inspired by his year-round daily commute from St. Adolphe to the Fort Garry area of Winnipeg. *If I can do it,* he thought, *why not others*? And what better inspiration than a race to challenge them?

The first ice bike race was held at The Forks in 1999 on a frozen and very slippery river surface with categories of five kilometres, ten kilometres, and twenty kilometres, which Daavid described as snowflake, icicle, and abominable, respectively.

One competitor recalled that the day was inordinately cold, even for

Manitoba Archives, Foote Collection N2641.

A ski jump and ski plane at River Park, January 1924.

Winnipeg with a biting north wind. It failed, however, to deter the forty-five participants and became an annual event.

Mountain biking on snow might provide an additional source of bicycle competition for those generally used to summertime conditions. A side benefit could be its inspiration for reluctant commuters, thus demonstrating how sports can be a positive force for tackling global warming.

New, more dramatic adaptations of skiing and skating are gaining increasing credibility. Downhill ice skating combined with a form of skatercross are one of the most popular events on Quebec City's winter events calendar. A 430-metre course down a sixty-metre drop starts from the city's historic Château Frontenac Hotel as skaters accelerate down through the city's old town on a course of man-made turns and bumps. All of this is staged at night to add to its drama as skaters crash into snowbanks and each other on their way to the finishing line.

Finally, a homegrown winter sport at which Canadians already excel has the extra advantage of its genuine First Nations roots. Snowsnake was played long before Europeans arrived in North America.

The snake itself is a long javelin-like hardwood pole about two to four metres long with its head shaped like a snake. A mixture of melted lead is poured into the nose. The "snake" is then tapered to a narrower tail. Grooves or notches allow it to be gripped by competitors. Different snow conditions often require that participants have access to a number of snakes as well as waxes to polish the wood, much like those used by cross-country skiers.

The snake is tossed, in a pendulum swinging-type motion, toward a wide "pitch hole" that tapers to a narrow and lengthy track through which the snowsnake passes often for a distance of a kilometre or more. The winner is the one who throws the snowsnake the farthest.

Rules, like those in other non-commercialized games, often varied from one community to the next. Early peoples who played the sport often superstitiously got rid of their snake in the spring for fear it might come to life, but today the sporting tool is favoured for its longevity, as well as its resiliency and performance.

While the above may seem to be unlikely candidates for inclusion, consider the case of ski cross, or ski racing, which replicates the skatercross spirit as four to six skiers compete on the same course, at the same time, against each other over a course featuring banked turns, uneven surfaces, fabulous jumps, and the occasional elbow and push between contenders. In 2006 the International Olympic Committee added ski cross to its Vancouver roster of events. It will feature thirty-two men and sixteen women competing in the same format as the snowboard version. The two gold medals awarded will bring the number of medal events in Vancouver to eighty-six. At the same time, Olympic officials rejected women's ski jumping, a sport that has been well established for years.

FIVE

Our International Glory and How Winter Sports Made It Possible

Every four years national pride rises as Canadians confront a winter season with a difference. It's an occasion for a number of sports that receive little fanfare (with the exception of hockey) to be on full display. It's a tradition that involves Canadians enthusiastically cheering on their new heroes in biathlon, speed skating, and bobsledding, amongst other sports. Canadians have had a marvellous Winter Olympics history that has helped cultivate their patriotism.

While Canada missed the first Summer Olympics in Athens in 1896, they actually achieved gold in winter sports four years before the first official Winter Olympics when the Winnipeg Falcons won hockey gold at the Antwerp Summer Games in 1920.

While we like to think we're masters of many winter events and indeed, the goal of owning the podium at the 2010 Games in Vancouver is setting a target of most medals by any nation, our pickings were slim prior to the Second World War. Only hockey provided gold from 1924 through 1932, with Canada represented chronologically by Toronto Granites, University of Toronto Grads, and Winnipeg. It was a string no

The Winnipeg Falcons, ice hockey gold medalists at the VII Olympiad in Antwerp in 1920 (hockey was included in the 1920 Summer Olympics before becoming part of the first Winter Olympics in 1924).

Manitoba Archives N5476.

one feared ending in 1936, but events were to prove otherwise.

The Olympic Games, both winter and summer of 1936, were notorious and the Summer Olympics in particular was perhaps the most controversial sporting event of the twentieth century for the manner in which Nazi Germany successfully used them to deflect attention from their militarist and racial policies, and legitimize their identity as the new face of Europe, not only for restoring German pride, but their apparent ability to overcome the crippling world depression through public works.

The Winter Olympics, held in the German resort of Garmisch-Partenkirchen earlier in the year, are not as well commented on despite the presence of over a thousand athletes from twenty-eight countries. It was here, however, that the Nazis refined their approach to the more important Summer Games.

Hitler and his henchmen Goering, Goebbels, and Hess were regular attendees. The German secret police at first overplayed their brutishness by bullying guests, but quickly learned how to manage potentially unruly situations. Just before the Games started, anti-Semitic signs on the roads leading to the resort were taken down following protests from Olympic officials that their presence violated Germany's promises and if no action was taken it might jeopardize their hosting both Games even at that late date. These offensive messages, and even more violent activities, returned after the two Olympics were completed, culminating November 9–10, 1938, in Kristallnacht or the Night of Broken Glass in which German Jews were murdered, twenty-five to thirty thousand were sent to concentration camps, and two hundred synagogues were destroyed. It was part of a Nazi policy leading to mass genocide.

The Games at Garmisch were further threatened by something over which the Fuhrer had no control — mild temperatures. But all that changed when the opening ceremonies were blanketed in wet snow. Controversy broke out immediately as Canada called for the banishment of two members of Great Britain's hockey team, Jimmy Foster and Alex Archer, because they had not received appropriate clearances from the Canadian teams for which they had played before jumping to the then-popular English club league.

The British team was made up of "native-borns" with the exception of Gerry Davey and Gordon Dailley, who, though Canadian by birth, had attained British residency. The "native-borns," however, had been prominent players in Canada, their families in most cases immigrating to Canada and their children growing up in a hockey-mad country.

For his part, as the leader of the American delegation, Avery Brundage, a stickler for amateur purity and an apologist for the German government of the day, supported the Canadian protest. "I'd just as soon only have to play one Canadian team," he said in reference to the challenge facing his United States hockey team.

After much behind-the-scenes wrangling in which E.A. Gilroy, the president of the Canadian Amateur Hockey Association, damned the English hockey league as nothing more than a racket (no doubt for its under the table payments to star players), Canada finally relented and withdrew its objections. It was a decision they would regret.

Canada did not seem overly concerned. In winning all four previous Olympic hockey tournaments, they had outscored their rivals, many of them novices to the game, by a combined score of 209–8.

Developments in Canada, however, may have been an early warning sign of trouble ahead. By rights, the 1935 Allan Cup champion Halifax

Wolverines should have represented Canada, but the loss of key players and squabbling over payment led instead to the selection of the Port Arthur Bearcats, runners-up to the Wolverines.

Behind the scenes, Labour, Jewish, and other progressive groups in the United States, Britain, and Canada had demanded that their countries boycott the German Games. This effort failed. Ominously on Boxing Day of 1935, however, the Bearcats hockey team was picketed by their own countrymen, members of the Winnipeg Trades and Labour Council, at an exhibition game raising money to send the hockey players overseas.

The SS *Duchess of Athol* left Halifax Harbour for Europe on January 18, 1936, with members of the Winter Olympic team on board. Signs had been painted on the side of the boat the night before declaring, "No Canucks to the Olympics," "Down With Fascism," and an appeal to free a German Communist leader.

Unsettling as these events might have been, the Canadian hockey team got off to a rousing start, winning all three of its first-round games. In the next round, however, the controversial British goalie, Jimmy Foster, from Winnipeg, though born in Scotland, proved that a hot goalie is one of the most dangerous opponents an overconfident team can play against. Despite constant pressure and several excellent goal-scoring opportunities, Canada lost to Britain 2–1.

Oh well, they must have thought, *we'll make up for that in the later final round*. However, it was not to be, as authorities ruled that having beaten a team once in the competition a second game against them was not required. This didn't guarantee the British the gold medal, as they still had other teams to beat, but for Canadians it meant victory was now out of their hands. Fury overtook the Canadian camp and it was even rumoured that the entire Olympic team might quit Germany.

Cooler heads prevailed somewhat and Canada eventually defeated Hungary. It was their next game with Germany, however, that aroused major passions.

Hockey had proved popular with Germany's leaders with Hitler himself attending Britain's game with Hungary. Germany's hockey team had one of Europe's best players, Rudi Ball, born in Berlin in 1910. Prior to these Games he had recently played in Italy and Switzerland. His

Cecil Smith, Canadian Olympian.

place in Germany's roster was one of the Games' most controversial. Ball was Jewish.

According to British papers Nazi Party members were disgusted, while on the other hand, a Jewish spokesperson decried Ball's acceptance of the offer.

Ball had been asked to join the team from his exile outside the country by the Reich sports leader Hans Von Tschammer Und Osten. This was less for Ball's obvious skills than for the party's desperate need to convince foreigners that Jewish athletes were not banned from participation if they met the standard of excellence. Deliberate roadblocks placed in the path of Jewish athletes put the lie to this claim, but Ball's participation allowed the Nazis to plead innocence.

Heavy snow falling on the tournament's outdoor surface constantly interrupted the game in which he played for Germany against the United States. It had to be regularly cleared and possibly its stop-and-start nature had an effect on him. In any case, he was eventually injured and missed his team's game with Canada. Given what happened that was just as well as his German supporters might have blamed him.

In Lewis Erenberg's 2006 book, *The Greatest Fight of Our Generation: Louis vs. Schmeling*, he claims that, "In *Mein Kampf*, Hitler argued that boxing and hockey would transform German youth into proper Aryans and future soldiers." A necessarily uncomfortable review of Hitler's book, however, found reference only to boxing and ju-jitsu as the key sports. The reference is possibly elsewhere in Hitler's writings.

In any case, Hitler's acolytes were eager attendees at Canada's match with Germany. This was the real test for their team because despite Canada's loss, most European squads measured themselves against them.

How can we know the real temperament of those Canadian players? Criticized by protesting countrymen in Canada, alarmed by the presence of players in Britain's lineup they considered illegitimate, annoyed by unpredictable ice conditions, not only affected by blowing snow but occasionally rendered sloppy by temperatures of up to 8°C, and finally realizing they would not get another chance against the Brits, mayhem must have been on their minds.

An article in the *Globe*'s February 14, 1936, issue is graphic in its description:

> Before a crowd of 10,000 plus thousands packed around the stadium, the Dominion hockey men dropped the gentleness that had marked earlier games

and gave the German team, the German populace, and German Government officials a lesson in the art of body checking. The bumps are perfectly legal but the opposing hockey men didn't like them and neither did the pro-German crowd.

German fans booed the Canadians and the American referee to no avail. This was not only Canadian revenge for perceived past injustices, but perhaps a not-too-subtle criticism of their German hosts. The third period started, in the words of the *Globe*, as a combination of hockey, shinny, and a donnybrook, as the German crowd, not used to seeing their countrymen abused in so public a manner, and aroused by their leaders to think of themselves as a Master Race, became increasingly agitated.

"At one time," the *Globe* wrote, "the demonstration was so pronounced Joseph Paul Goebbels, German Minister for Propaganda, arose in the official box and motioned for the crowd to cease. Goebbels was a colorful picture, dressed in the costume of Daniel Boone. He was accompanied by Herman Goering, Minister for Air, and other dignitaries."

We can only wish Leni Riefenstahl had been there to record this game and its extraordinary character for history as she did in Berlin in creating the official Olympic film, to this day regarded as one of the great works of motion picture art.

Canada's last hope was an American victory over Britain, but after three overtime periods, officials finally called that game with the score still tied 0–0. Britain won the gold medal. Canada took home silver and fell victim to one of greatest upsets in Olympic history, offset only by the realization that essentially a bunch of Canucks had done the improbable on behalf of the country in which they had been born.

Congratulatory messages were sent from Canada to their British cousins, ties to the old country still being too strong to elicit greater furor. Reuters, however, reported that, "Canadians believe that the native-born Englishman has no natural facilities for the game, whereas Canadian children play ice hockey from the age of four onwards." The wire service warned that E.A. Gilroy faced hard questions on his return from Germany following his handling of the situation regarding the reinstated British players.

Manitoba Archives, Foote Collection N1934.

Emile St. Godard, 1932 Winter Olympian in Lake Placid, New York, February 2, 1927.

As for Rudi Ball, he survived the war, switched from right wing to defence late in a career that lasted into early 1950s, won three Spengler Cups during his career (an honour still sought by countries including Canada), and died in Johannesburg, South Africa, in 1975.

Only one other Canadian won silver in this pre-war period, Alex Hurd in the men's 1,500-metre speed skating in 1932, where he was joined on the podium by bronze medalist William Logan. Cecil Elaine Smith was the first Canadian female to compete in the Winter Olympics at the age of fifteen in 1924, doing so in both Ladies and Pairs figure skating. She returned to the Olympics in 1928, but failed to medal.

Another prominent female athlete of the era, Lela Brooks, competed in three demonstration speed-skating events at the 1932 Games in Lake Placid. Indicative perhaps of the Games' still-emerging popularity, Brooks qualified for the 1936 Games, but chose to get married instead.

The Lake Placid Games were dogged by unpredictable weather and truckloads of snow were shipped in from the north so that when Emile

St. Godard won the eighty-kilometre demonstration dogsled race he did it at least partly on Canadian snow.

Arguably, Canada's greatest Olympic achievement belongs to Barbara Ann Scott and her capturing of the women's figure-skating gold medal at the 1948 St. Moritz Winter Olympics.

Why? She was a world champion and the dominant performer in the immediate postwar period, but all too often such a pedigree can be an impediment for an athlete on the world's biggest stage.

In 1948 the Olympics were the biggest stage. Today they are surrounded by high-profile televised events and athletes can amass a small fortune on the basis of even a mediocre career. Not so in the 1940s when the world was in recovery not only from war, but a devastating depression.

Barbara Ann Scott was a beacon of Canadian hope that brighter days were, if not already there, then just around the corner. She had a petite figure and a compelling innocence appealing to both women and men, young and old. Canada hadn't won a Winter Olympic gold since 1932, so they were ready to celebrate.

However, Scott's greatest appeal was perhaps her extraordinary coolness in the face of pressure that would have shattered others. Hers was a sporting focus that psychologists are only now beginning to acknowledge as the successful athlete's supreme strength. When the margins of performance and those of potential error between competitors are so small and luck can rearrange even the best-laid plans, it is the athlete's ability to shut out the outside world and totally concentrate on the challenge at hand that ultimately shapes their success or failure.

Barbara Ann Scott went to the Winter Olympics as the favourite, so much so that the malevolent American Olympic official Avery Brundage queried Scott as to whether she would talk to him after he was behind an investigation into the awarding of a car to her after a world championship victory. It could have resulted in her disqualification from amateur and therefore Olympic competition.

"How strange," she later said innocently, "because I couldn't conceive of not speaking to someone to whom I've been introduced."

Then he asked if she had won the gold medal, an absurd question since her event had not started, but perhaps an attempt to put her off by implying that self-assurance could be her fatal flaw. Her only thought was that this was such a curious exchange.

Warm weather and the use of the rink for hockey made ice conditions on the open-air rink far from ideal. Twenty-five women competed in Barbara's event and had arrived at the rink for a 7:30 a.m. start to their school figures. Water stood on the ice. Only one figure was completed before judges ruled that conditions would not allow for further competition that day.

More sun and warmth prevented the now anxious athletes from competing the next day. Scott was pragmatic. She had practised perhaps twenty-thousand hours in preparation and waited so long for this moment. One more day was no problem for her, but possibly not for others.

It got a little colder overnight, but the ice was still questionable. During her "loop change loop" manoeuvre, the ice was buzzed by a low-flying plane that hid Scott's tracing from her. Then, as her routine drew to a close, a gaggle of photographers and newsreel men invaded the ice close to where she was finishing. Only her ability to totally concentrate on what she was doing got her through these potential disasters.

The weather had backed up the Olympic schedule and two hockey games were played on the same ice on which the women would have to do their freestyle routine. By the time the women went on there were ruts and holes all over the ice. A preceding skater, Eileen Seigh, warned Scott that the ice was terrible.

The water hadn't frozen and despite attempts to sluice off the liquid all it did was hide the poor condition of the ice. "Play it safe, not spectacular," Seigh warned. Ice was good only at the ends of the rink and Scott quickly revised her program to complete her most difficult jumps and spins in those areas.

Canadian hockey players who would themselves win gold lifted Barbara Ann Scott on their shoulders when her winning point total was announced. The country celebrated as it only occasionally has the opportunity to do, and Scott, who would be celebrated by the prime minister and through ticker tape parades, had become a Canadian winter sports legend.

In 1952 the Edmonton Mercurys won gold in hockey, but no one would have guessed that such a feat would not be repeated by another Canadian team for fifty years. Four years later Canada was shut out of gold entirely as Frances Dafoe and Norris Bowden missed gold by the narrowest of margins in figure-skating pairs.

Barbara Paul and Bob Wagner finally got the pairs gold in 1960 along with Anne Heggtveit in women's slalom skiing.

Four years later Canadian men were deprived of a bronze medal in hockey on the basis of goal differential. There was greater success however in bobsledding.

Canada's involvement with this sport may not suggest its "fish out of water" character. The movie *Cool Runnings* has put that narrative to good use with its story of a team from Jamaica attempting to compete in the Winter Olympics. But Canada's bobsledding saga is one that arguably could be considered more improbable and dramatic than that of the Jamaican team, for the simple reason that Canada won.

The story unfolded in 1964 at the Olympics in Innsbruck, Austria. It was the first time Canadians had competed at the Olympic level. They were huge underdogs. The Austrians had a proud history in the event, and the advantage of having it in their home country, and at their facilities. The Canadian story has evolved through the years, but even from this distance in time the victory is still shocking.

Over the years they have been portrayed as a bunch of partying Canadians who somehow made their way to the Olympic Village in Innsbruck and then fluked their way to victory by just jumping in their bobsled and somehow getting down the track on the required four trips, faster than anyone else. In truth, members of the team, Peter Kirby, Douglas Anakin, John Emery and Vic Emery, were all extremely intelligent, and put that to use. They weren't simply partying ski bums who somehow fell into a bobsled and went down a hill.

In fact, the team was quickly given the nickname "the intellectual sled" by their competition. With no bobsled track in Canada, the team trained diligently before the Games in a gymnasium and did some trials at Lake Placid. However, despite their intelligence, and unique training style, they were still extraordinary long shots to defeat the mighty Austrians.

Jack McCulloch of Winnipeg, Manitoba — amateur champion of the world having defeated Harold Hagan of Norway in an international meet at Montreal in 1897 in the years before the opportunity to compete in the Winter Olympics.

In their first time down the track, the Canadian team stunned the crowds by producing a track record. They followed with another impressive run, and another, and by the time all the runs were complete, the Canadian bobsled team, in the country's first-ever appearance in the event, had won a gold medal.

Canada's initial success with the bobsled was followed by years of mediocrity. With an advancing field of skilled bobsledders from other nations competing, combined with the lack of facilities for Canadian bobsledders, Canada was a virtual non-player until they created a more sophisticated track for the 1988 Calgary Winter Olympics. With these new facilities in place, Canadians returned to the top of the podium in the 1998 Nagano Games where Pierre Lueders and Dave MacEachern won in the two-man bobsled.

Four years after the bobsled victory, another Canadian went to the Games with the opposite challenge. As an odds-on favourite, skier Nancy Greene did not disappoint, bringing home gold and silver medals from Grenoble, France. Greene was a very popular figure amongst Canadians leading up to the Olympics, having been named Canada's Athlete of the Year in 1967.

Greene's accomplishments in Grenoble included a gold medal performance in the giant slalom, posting one of the largest margins of victory in Olympic history, along with silver in the slalom. Greene's impressive showing was highlighted by her overcoming an ankle injury just weeks before the Olympics.

She went on to endorse commercial products such as Mars Bars, ushering in a now common opportunity for Canadian winter athletes. She and her husband developed a new ski area in the Whistler region of British Columbia, site of many 2010 winter events. In 1999, a poll conducted amongst newspaper editors and broadcasters by the Canadian Press voted her along with Wayne Gretzky as Canada's female and male athletes of the twentieth century. In 2008 she was appointed to the Canadian Senate by Prime Minister Stephen Harper.

The next few Olympics were relatively lean for Canada with Kathy Kreiner taking gold in the women's giant slalom in 1976, the only first place in a year in which Montreal hosted the Summer Olympics, and where Canada became the first host nation not to win gold. It was a record sadly repeated at Calgary's hosting of the Winter Games in 1988. In 1984, however, Gaetan Boucher took home two golds in men's speed skating, while Brian Orser's silver in men's figure skating was repeated again four year later.

Hosting the 1988 Games in Calgary was a monumental moment for Canada's Winter Olympic athletes. It allowed the country to create facilities later used by Canadian athletes to train for future Games. Calgary built numerous state-of-the-art facilities for speed skating, cross-country skiing, the bobsled, and the Nakiska Alpine Ski Area. It also produced the Olympic Saddledome, which provided Calgary with a new home for their National Hockey League team, the Flames. It may be a major reason a team still exists in Calgary in light of other Canadian teams in Winnipeg and Quebec having to move to the United States due to inadequate facilities.

Calgary's hosting of the Olympics was a collective triumph for the city and the country as a whole. The experience brought tremendous excitement and some anxiety leading up to the event. It put Calgary in the international spotlight for the first time as something other than the home of the annual Stampede. There were some controversies, including opportunists gouging visitors seeking accommodation.

These problems aside, by most objective standards the Games were considered a success. The federal government contributed $225 million, Alberta $125 million and Calgary added another $50 million. This accounted for half of the total budget, with the other half provided through sponsorships, licensing, and broadcasting rights.

A side effect of the Calgary Games was an indoor Olympic speed-skating oval, part of the continuing trend of moving outdoor events into climate-controlled environments.

Elizabeth Manley and Brian Orser's figure-skating silvers were highlights for Canada, though the disappointment of no gold was pronounced, a fact still remembered in ads for the 2010 Games with the promise to end that hometown drought.

Canada's Winter Olympic fortunes began to turn around in 1992 with Kerrin Lee-Gartner's downhill gold being one of the more notable events.

The Newfoundland Hockey Club, a national team before joining Confederation in 1949.

Two years later the Games returned as the decision had been made to stagger Winter and Summer Games so one of them would always appear within a two-year period. For Myriam Bédard it was a blessing, as she won two golds in biathlon.

A bounty of victories followed in 1998 and again in 2002 with Catriona Le May Doan and Marc Gagnon both winning gold medals for speed skating (Le May Doan in long track and Gagnon in short track). Snowboarding made its first appearance at Nagano, Japan in 1998, and Ross Rebagliati became its first gold medalist and then the first Olympian to be temporarily stripped of a medal for testing positive for having marijuana in his circulatory system.

The decision was challenged and, to Rebagliati's joy, was overturned. It was ruled that marijuana was not considered a performance-enhancing drug, and furthermore was not listed as a banned substance under Olympic rules. With egg on their face, the IOC added marijuana to their list of banned substances for the 2000 Summer Games in Sydney. It was dubbed by some as "the Ross Rebagliati rule."

The Canadian men's hockey team competing in 1998 was, for the first time, made up the nation's best players from the National Hockey League, including Wayne Gretzky. Fans stayed up into the wee hours of morning for the semifinal match in which they were defeated by the Czech Republic, who went on to win gold. A crushed Team Canada then lost the bronze medal playoff game to finish without even a visit to the podium. Canadian women also failed in their hockey gold medal quest after one of the team's stars, Angela James, was left at home.

Therefore, in 2002 hockey gold for both Canadian men and women symbolized the country's supremacy in a sport they once dominated at these games.

More strangely, two apparent silver and bronze medals in those 2002 Salt Lake City Games were later upgraded.

No story attracted more attention than that of the figure-skating pair of Jamie Salé and David Pelletier, who eventually shared gold medals with Russian skaters Bereznaya and Sikharulidze after one of the most bizarre and controversial endings in an Olympic event.

Leading up to the Games in Salt Lake City, Jamie Salé and David Pelletier were strong contenders to bring Canada home a gold medal. Canadians were excited about the pair's routine for the 2002 Games, but were painfully aware that their success would not be easy. Salé and Pelletier were up against a formidable Russian pair. The Russians had a strong history in pairs figure skating.

In their long program, Salé and Pelletier riveted the American audience in the crowd, and millions watching on television screens across Canada. Canadian and American commentators were convinced it was a gold-medal performance from the Canadian pair, especially since the Russians had not skated a clean program. However, when the scores appeared, Salé and Pelletier were given second place by the majority of judges, 5–4, and thus, shockingly, Salé and Pelletier were whisked onto the podium, with the Russian national anthem playing to the stunned

American crowd, and given a silver medal.

Canadians were bewildered. And because the Games were taking place in the United States, the American media pounced on the controversy, digging deeper to see if there was more to the story. The day after the controversy began, French judge Marie-Reine Le Gougne confirmed that she had worked with the Russians to rig the judging for the event, in exchange for their co-operation in rigging the ice-dancing event for the French.

The fallout from the controversy led to suspensions of judges and officials who had their fingerprints on this backdoor dealing. Ultimately, Le Gougne's vote was thrown out, which meant the Canadians and Russians had tied in voting. Later in the week, Salé and Pelletier were awarded gold medals.

The entire storyline was front and centre on newscasts throughout North America for the entire 2002 Games, and made Salé and Pelletier more famous than they would ever have been had the controversy not erupted. They became instant celebrities and superstars both in Canada and the United States and they found themselves appearing on the *Today Show* and *Saturday Night Live*.

Likewise, Beckie Scott went from bronze to gold in women's cross-country skiing after the two competitors in front of her were adjudged to have used illegal substances. However, it took two years to resolve this issue.

At the Turin Winter Olympics Canada had its best Games in the country's history, winning twenty-four medals (seven gold, ten silver, and seven bronze), surpassing the previous high of seventeen set in 2002 and finishing third in the medal total. Notable golds were won by the Canadian men's curling team based out of Newfoundland, and the women's hockey team. Lascelles Brown became the first Jamaican-born Canadian to win a medal at the Winter Olympics as part of the Canadian two-man bobsled team, which finished second.

There is a certain charm to these Canadian athletic stories. The Winter Olympics have offered many relatively unknown Canadians an opportunity to become household names. Every four years, new names emerge, new celebrities are born, and more historical lore is added to Canada's story.

The Winter Olympics over the years have served as a canvas for Canadian athletes, to display their talents, to be observed by people all over the world, and over time becoming a part of Canada's rich culture. There are many other stories yet to be written as it is clear that the winter has been very kind to Canadians. It's a season with which Canadians have built a lovely friendship.

SIX

Ice Hockey in Legend, History, and Modern Times

Hockey is Canadian. There is no need for us to put the word "ice" in front of it. We don't need to distinguish it, as Europeans and others do, from the "field" version. Is it only natural, therefore, to conclude that Canadians invented hockey? Such is the slippery slope of historical investigation that we might not want to know the answer.

What in any case does "invent" mean? Creating something literally from nothing, out of a pure "eureka" moment in one's head? It sometimes seems our understanding is no more advanced than a comic book notion, whose best exemplar was Gyro Gearloose, first appearing alongside Donald Duck in the early 1950s. A light bulb would suddenly flash over Gearloose's head in a moment of inspiration. What had never been before was suddenly there, having been "invented."

Games, despite the wish of myth makers to pinpoint that "eureka" moment, are generally not formed this way. Instead they have a long and often lost pedigree of evolution. With reference to baseball's supposed "invention," historian John Thorn has said (and this could apply to hockey as well), "It's no more useful an idea than driving a stake into the

The St. Catharines Orioles of the Niagara District Hockey League, circa 1936. The Orioles were one of many all-Black hockey teams that prospered in southern Ontario and in Atlantic Canada in the first half of the twentieth century.

middle of a flowing body of water and declaring that this is where the river starts."

Even basketball, a modern game created by James Naismith in a Springfield, Massachusetts, gymnasium in 1893 owed at least some of its spirit and style to a popular folk game of "Duck on the Pond" that Naismith played as a child in Almonte, Ontario.

Hockey, following the general rule of most contemporary games, was eventually formalized by means of rules, organizational structure, the deadly seriousness of its participants, and many prescribed qualities from clothing to the price of tickets, but only after a long period of informal play had brought it to a point where "order" was necessary.

Montreal and Halifax took the leadership in applying their distinct interpretations to what was essentially a folk game with roots in dozens of still to be untangled forms including shinty, hurley, and perhaps even Russian bandy.

Fred. W. Grant recalled the games he played on the frozen ponds and lakes around Barrie:

Every kid carried a shinny — and knew how to use it, too.

"Shinny!" Say there isn't a man living who spent his boyhood days in Barrie forty years ago (circa 1880); to whom that word shinny doesn't bring back a whole brigade of happy memories. Shinny was a game that didn't need any rules — there wasn't any referee and there wasn't any captain, and no admission fee to look at someone else playing (imagine anyone standing on the ice looking at a shinny game!) — everyone was in the game. The goals were placed wherever they happened to be, and the goalpost might be an old tin can that had served as a puck before someone else produced something better, or a pile of overcoats discarded during the game, and they were separated anything from ten yards to ten miles, according to the circumstances.

One "side" might have twenty players and the other 220. That was merely incidental — everyone "knocked" whichever way he wanted to — who cared? The "hockey sticks" were anything from an old umbrella handle to a picket torn off a nearby fence and inverted to get a right slant on the ice, or anything else that would get results. But a maple or beech shinny fashioned according to each individual kid's own standard and cut from some sapling out in the swamp was the general weapon. The puck might be a doorknob, or a rubber ball, or an old boot heel, hardwood knot, or round stone picked up on the beach. And then the game started. When someone thought he was getting the short end of it, and hollered about it, the only satisfaction he derived was the passing advice thrown over the shoulder of the aggressor as he went after someone else. "Well, shinny on your own side!"

It was a game open to all ages and both sexes, at least judging by a Toronto *Globe* article of November 17, 1886, in its "Woman's World" column. The unnamed female writer appealed to her readers, "You climbed apple trees and fences and tore your clothes and raced and rioted and had as generally good and uproarious a time as your brothers had. Perhaps you even played hockey with them — I did, with crooked sticks and wrinkled horse chestnuts …"

A game without boundaries and limits on the number of players is pure folk and if there's anything characteristic of modern sport it is its imitation of how the English countryside had been removed from its common use for everything from tending crops to playing games. Sports' own enclosure movement required the defined space of the rink, even when played outdoors, as it was for many years at the Winter Olympics, and in more recent outdoor regular season games played by National Hockey League teams in Edmonton, Buffalo, and Chicago. As well, there were limits on the number of players, beginning with seven, but later reduced to six (and, at times five when the game introduced its regular-season overtime practice).

Two versions competed for this modernizing supremacy.

In the Nova Scotia game, early goalmouths ran parallel to the sides of what passed for a rink and players could score from either side. You didn't want to be a goalie in those days! In its favour, however, was a more liberal policy of forward passing.

Its rival, the Montreal game, had a more limiting offside rule and so its better players often rushed from one end of the ice to the other rather than passing backwards and therefore toward one's own net. Its most talented early practitioner was Cyclone Taylor, of whom it was said he once guarded the puck by skating backwards the length of the ice and scoring.

In later years he somewhat denied the story, saying, "It's a bit of a myth. Far be it for me to say yes or no that it happened, but it's a story that will go on and on into centuries to come." All sports are popularized by such tales.

The Montreal game became the dominant form and in the process snatched some of the better innovations from the Halifax game, such as the forward pass. Why was Montreal successful? As the leading Canadian city of the nineteenth century and well into the twentieth, it was Canada's cultural leader and mercantile centre. In brief, it had the power and authority to overcome the pretensions of less glamourous places.

Author's collection.

"Canadian Winter Sports: A Ladies' Hockey Team, Toronto, Canada."

In the same manner, of course, baseball, also a game with no inventor (despite claimants for Abner Doubleday and Cooperstown), was effectively modernized in New York City, the trend-setting centre not only of the United States, but also in large measure of North America and, increasingly, beyond.

However, the Society for International Hockey Research (SIHR) has in some ways fought a rearguard action against the claim of Windsor, Nova Scotia, to be the game's birthplace. Those first off the mark in declaring their primacy often have the advantage of non-critical appraisal by a media keen to declare a first for anything. Windsor has been particularly opportunistic.

Their claim is based largely on a fictional account from Thomas Chandler Haliburton's novel *The Attaché, or Sam Slick in England* in which the author says, through the mouthpiece of his fictional American protagonist Sam Slick , "And you boys let out racin', yelpin', hollerin', and whoopin' like mad with pleasure, and the playground, and the game of bass in the fields, or hurly on the long pond on the ice."

Windsor's promoters argue that while fictional, it refers to

Haliburton's own youth as a school boy at King's College in Windsor from which he graduated in 1815.

It's not much to go on and the SIHR researchers thought so in their report, which noted that even if a fictional account could be corroborated as an actual remembrance (which in this case it can't) it would not be the first time such a game had been recorded, there being many European paintings and accounts describing something to us that looks like hockey on ice. As well Haliburton's fiction makes no mention of skates, a rather important element of the game, one would agree!

And even if a hockey-type game had been played at this time in this place, it is significant only if it then transfers to other locales and becomes the starting point from which our current enthusiasm and the structured game date. Once again it fails on that account with Kingston and Montreal being far better positioned to make such a claim.

So that should have put the matter to rest, but while it was shown long ago that Cooperstown had nothing to do with baseball's origins other than some limited records of folk-type games played there in the early part of the nineteenth century (and no different from accounts in other places around the same time or earlier), its myth continues to this day. In fact, in holding on to their claim the Windsor folks might be too modest by half; for the Haliburton fictional account says the lads were also playing "bass in the fields," suggesting that an equally spurious, but determined claim by them could be made for baseball's creation.

Hockey was played at least in primitive form in Europe before it arrived in North America. We have pictorial evidence for this as far back as the sixteenth century. There is good reason, as well, to suggest that its development in Canada was matched in the northeast United States as shown in a painting by John O'Toole of a skating scene from around 1835 in which skaters are using sticks for hockey-type purpose.

Following the logic of the Windsor claim, with its foundation in fiction, one might even suggest that the words from the mouth of Haliburton's fictional American Sam Slick, as to boys playing hockey in Windsor, were based on that fictional character's awareness of such games in the United States and that he simply transferred them to Nova Scotia for the benefit of his (also fictional) travelling companion Squire

Manitoba Archives.

The Brandon Eight ladies' hockey team, circa 1898.

Poker. However, this requires a level of internal deconstruction that we'll not pursue any further.

Nevertheless, one thing is clear about the way modern games develop. At first they are an idle recreation for the common people of villages and rural settlements whose occupations are tied to the land and service to others. They have characteristics we call "folk" for the way they are embedded in people's everyday life without any consideration of the meaning or value they might have in their own right. There were no formal teams, standings, or league structure, and only the most basic of playing standards, which we might call rules, and which varied from one village to another even those perhaps a few miles apart.

As often as not these folk customs were rooted in earlier religious rites whose origins in some cases predate written history. They began as an extension of a complete religious ceremony, but as they became increasingly sophisticated they often assumed a life of their own. We can see some of this evolutionary character in a study of the Native game of lacrosse, which was significantly connected to First Nations belief systems, but also was able to stand at least partially on its own two feet as a ritualized activity for healing, gambling, and preparation for warfare.

Likewise, the discovery of a primitive form of baseball in the North African desert by an Italian anthropologist, Corrado Gini, in the 1930s shed light on the origin of bat-and-ball games as an element of fertility worship and a celebration of spring's return. There remain types of football, as well, with folk and quasi-religious roots, the best known being Derbyshire football played on the day before Ash Wednesday between two English villages.

Hockey was no different. It seems possible that it might have had its structured origin in Europe if only the climate been more conducive to the annual repetition of the game. But examples from Dutch ponds or the English fens, while fascinating, fail to suggest anything other than one-off recreations for the simple reason that annual freezing conditions were not guaranteed.

Think how joyous it must have been to play this folk game of shinty or hurley on ice during one particularly cold winter, but then how disappointing to the point of forgetfulness, to be unable to return to that unique sport for perhaps another ten or more years. An entire generation of playing would be lost and the foundation, on which the game might have grown, in the way cricket did in the eighteenth century, was lost.

Now transfer that dimly remembered play to North America, where winter is long and cold. Climate change did not as yet have the industrial revolution and carbon releases to further distort the weather system. The shock of winter's cold, particularly to Europeans experiencing it for the first time in North America, must have been pronounced.

It was either stay inside for months on end or find a way to survive winter as enjoyably as possible. The folk game of shinty, or hurley on ice, was a perfect response. Owing to its folk origins, however, this game was not as yet taken seriously. It was played much in the manner as it is by children today — an informal pick-up type of play with the group's own interpretation of the general guidelines and with no concern for the result. It certainly wasn't fodder for newspaper stories.

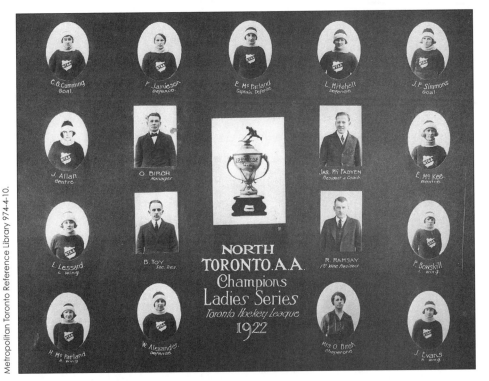

The North Toronto Athletic Association's Ladies' Series champions, 1922.

Possibly its strong folk character held back its more rapid development as other sports prospered in Canada. Lacrosse, with its First Nations heritage, was usurped and quickly "modernized" by European settlers. Cricket and curling arrived in Canada as basically fully fledged modern games. Snowshoeing had no folk-game character, being a strictly utilitarian endeavour and so was easily turned into competitive sport and recreation. While baseball's folk character shared an English, American, Canadian, and even a Germanic background, it made its leap to serious form in the United States.

With so many sporting rivals it's not overly surprising that we find no formal recognition of hockey, other than its sporadic, and almost accidental, mention in unrelated news accounts and diaries, in the period up to, and for many years after, Canada's 1867 Confederation.

Games of "the unwashed" can reside below the surface of serious reporting, organization, and popular consideration for years, in a kind of cultural backwater. Hockey on ice as it slowly evolved in nineteenth-century Canada nevertheless was laying down an important foundation, which we, at a distance of over a century and a half in some cases, can only vaguely glimpse.

Perhaps as was the case with baseball in its early years, hockey in Canada was seen as essentially a rube's game. Folk customs being identified with the less well-educated members of a pre-industrial society, anyone continuing their practice in the supposedly modern age might be looked upon as somewhat immature in their behaviour.

A game's formal organization into a modern serious sport is usually at the behest of the elite. They legitimize what appears to most people to be a somewhat lowbrow (folk and middling class) entertainment. Elite members of society are less likely to be laughed at and, as cultural trendsetters, any mockery they experience is short-lived (and if not, the phenomenon is abandoned).

For the upper class, organized sports serve several purposes. In the nineteenth century they fed a doctrine of muscular Christianity, in which Herbert Spencer's "survival of the fittest," alongside ideas of moral superiority, were never far from the surface. They also provided useful social networking opportunities, a function never abandoned. For others they were simply a useful venue for gambling, but for which uniform rules were necessary if contests were to take place with at least the pretense of a level playing field.

Ironically, this elite usually gives the sport back to its one-time folk adherents (polo might be an exception), now largely an urban working class, who in turn adopt it with an enthusiasm for its structure, rules, culture, and strict amateur/professional distinctions that they might once have laughed at, or rejected, when it was "their" game.

The timing of this return of the game to its popular base is often uneven. Cricket only grudgingly accepted working-class participation and retained a sharp distinction between the elite, usually dubbed gentlemen and by definition also amateurs, and its lowbrow participants, for whom it was a paid profession, until well into the twentieth century. Organized hockey, on the other hand, was almost immediately returned as a formalized activity to the broader, "unwashed," society in whose

The Davisville Hockey Club, 1911 or 1912, at the current location of the Davisville subway station in Toronto.

realm it had been percolating throughout the century.

Amateur and professional squabbles continued well into the twentieth century. The early history of all modern sport has many accounts of those from working-class or First Nations communities whose lives were damaged by this cruel distinction. In the case of hockey, however, the game was too well entrenched in its folk form to dissuade participants from worrying about these occasional wrangles.

Seemingly out of nowhere, a game neglected in media accounts burst on the public scene in the last two decades of the 1800s. D. Burke Simpson, the most prominent lawyer in the town of Bowmanville in the last half of the nineteenth century, was one of the attendees at the first organizational meeting for the Ontario Hockey Association in 1890, yet one finds no mention of the game in his town's newspaper, *The Canadian Statesman*, until several years later. Why the delay?

While the game had been played informally it had yet to reach a level of popular acceptance.

Likewise in Toronto, hockey suddenly drew significant attention in the 1890s, but this was many years after its famous account in Montreal on March 3, 1875, at the Victoria Skating Rink. This reference is often cited as evidence of the game's public arrival and organizational legitimacy. It is notable for being what the SIHR Origins Committee calls, "... the earliest eyewitness account known, at least to this SIHR committee, of a specific game of hockey in a specific place at a specific time, and with a recorded score, between two identified teams."

One of the more curious comments in this Montreal account, however, is the Montreal *Gazette*'s additional note that, "Hockey though much in vogue on the ice in New England and other parts of the United States, is not known much here." While this might demonstrate the writer's ignorance, it also suggests the game had not yet reached a level of public awareness in Montreal.

Canada firsters might cautiously examine the game's records in the United States with more diligence in an attempt to understand what influence its rise there might have had in Canada. For instance, the first professional league in 1909 was in the United States so that country is owed a larger debt of gratitude than is commonly offered.

Given this apparent popularity in the United States and, of course Montreal, what accounts for the game's delay in reaching Toronto? There are many possible explanations.

Perhaps that city's elite had other winter games to occupy their time, including curling, which was very popular in southern Ontario. And Toronto winters were not as long as those of Montreal, nor could natural ice conditions be guaranteed. Hockey had been played informally, but records are sparse as to how widespread. One of the more curious accounts is a letter to the editor of the *Globe* in December 1862 about skaters being attacked on the Don River by "young rowdies" with shinty sticks. It seems unlikely that these youth didn't also play games with these sticks, nor likely they were slipping and sliding on the ice of the Don without the benefit of skates. They may have been embittered by the "swells" whose skating parties interrupted their rough-and-tumble matches.

A ladies' hockey team in Bowmanville, Ontario, 1924. They represented Bowmanville in the Ladies' Lakeshore League. Back row: Mansfield Cook, Maude Wilcox Elford, Bessie Kilgannon Donoghue, Alma Piper Cole, Nora Cluff, Gladys Mutton, Gordon Richards; front row: Hattie Seymour Armstrong, Mildred Luxton Edmondson, Nell Piper Wilson.

Nevertheless, such a group of common toughs was hardly a foundation for making primitive hockey popular. By their very nature they indicate the rough-hewn nature of its first adherents, as well as the incredible gestation period necessary for a game to raise its profile to a level from which the better schools and professional societies could take over as they did in the 1890s.

Having reached that tipping point of acceptance by the 1890s, the game exploded in popularity and was taken west with many of the first emigrants from eastern Canada. The 1896 Moose Jaw Ice Carnival featured a gala week of hockey and curling. The Moose Jaw hockey boys, as they were called, avenged an earlier defeat to Medicine Hat, while Regina won a fast game against "the Hat." Poetry flowed in the Regina *Leader* of March 12, 1896:

Come, cross your sticks upon the ice,
The air is keen, the watchers wait,
And eager as a cat for mice
About the puck the forwards skate!
Line up! In goal! The game is faced.
The puck's in play, the ice doth ring
Beneath the steel that seems to sing:
We have no time tonight to waste!
Away! Away! The high roof rings
And echoes with our buoyant mirth!
From side to side each party flings
Winged wit that mocks the other's worth!
And blue eyes shine with flashing pride,
And cheeks are red, and teeth a gleam
And 'kerchiefs wave and fair ones scream
To see the forwards dash and glide!
Fleet mercury goes hand in hand
With zero through the air tonight;
They write their names upon the land,
They set their seal on windows white.
But here our pulse beats high and warm,
So swift and keen the flashing game!
Twould set old Zero's half a-flame,
And take his frigid heart by storm.

The game was flourishing amongst all levels of Canadian society. A Colored Hockey League for Atlantic Canada's Black population was in place by the start of the new century. Women, from the governor general's family to the working class, played the game. A Toronto *Globe* story of January 30, 1893, described the formal splendour of a drawing room event for five hundred ladies and gentlemen in the Senate chamber: "The rapidity with which the bowing operations were got through with was marvelous, owing, it is said, to the anxiety of his excellency to attend the hockey match between the Ottawa and Montreal teams at the Rideau rink."

A hockey team at Villa de Lion in Dawson, Yukon Territory, circa 1900.

Francophone Canadians took to the game alongside their Anglophone neighbours. The often acrimonious, but always evolving, dialogue as to alternative futures fuels the country's language duality. On one thing that both English and French language speakers agree upon, however, is the primacy of hockey. One might say a country needs more than that to ensure its resiliency to tangled disputes, but on the other hand, it has not been a bad meeting place for cultural rapprochement. In the National Hockey League's early days, two teams contested for the affection of Montrealers, les Canadiens amongst Francophones, and the Maroons for the city's Anglophone community. The latter team, however, disappeared after the 1938 season, a victim of the Depression, but also perhaps the decision of English-speaking Montrealers to invest their cheering future with the Francophone-identified team.

As it was relatively late in the nineteenth century in achieving public recognition, hockey drew inspiration and ideas from two well-established sports, lacrosse and rugby — games in which physical contact and, in some cases, violence is pronounced. Hockey borrowed the idea of offside from rugby and even the design of its early shirts. From lacrosse it took much of that game's leadership, and its occasionally brutal character.

Lacrosse's decline in Ontario in the early twentieth century, like that of snowshoeing in Montreal, is at least partly attributable to this flight of its top players and organizers from one sport to another. In November 1886, the first twelve of the Toronto Lacrosse Club had decided to form a hockey club, "with a view," they said, "to keeping the active members of the club in playing shape during the winter months." By 1896, however, lacrosse players who played hockey in the winter were, according to accounts of the day, "... experts on the ice and it is likely that from among them enough good material can be found to form a first-class hockey seven."

While lacrosse's generally violent character had been deplored for years it made an easy jump to the newly popular game of hockey, rearing its head immediately. A Granites versus Wanderers match in Toronto featured Charley Thompson being carried out almost insensible after being "crushed against the wall," Mel Lucas had a tooth knocked out, and W. Harstone was stunned "by a chance blow to the face," all reported in the Toronto *Globe* on January 28, 1892, which then editorialized, "Another such exhibition of brutality ... would kill the sport of hockey in short order." Never was a prediction more off base than this one.

The *Globe* reported on January 29, 1894, how little Edward Dinwoodie died from a blow to the head from a hockey stick in the hands of a fellow player. The January 6, 1896, Toronto *Star* reported that Smith of the Ottawa team had to be escorted from a Montreal rink "under guard to save him from violence." Four days later the *Star* further described how Johnson and Forsyth started a fight early in the Granites versus Victorias match. "Some spectators interfered and held Forsyth; then his team rushed to the rescue, so did the Granites, and in a moment a large part of the crowd surged on the ice. There was swearing and scuffling on all sides, and the scene was disgraceful."

In response the Ontario Hockey Association resolved to suspend players who engaged in rough play. "This decision," the *Star* reported on January 17, 1896, "will be hailed with delight by all true lovers of the game, who like to see science, not rowdyism." It was a conclusion not supported by the game's future evolution.

The game for all its brutality, proved to be amazingly resilient in transcending the regional peculiarities of Canada, reaching the west coast by the turn of the century, but frustrating its adherents by virtue of that region's lack of consistent freezing conditions. Not to be outdone, denizens of Victoria put their minds to modernizing a system of artificial ice, thus removing the last barrier to the game's unpredictability. In the process this allowed the game to return to its European roots where it also flourished in the twentieth century.

Not that everyone was happy with this newly modernized game of hockey in comparison to its robust, freewheeling days on frozen ponds. Writing from Victoria in 1920, Fred W. Grant said:

> Of that old shinny playing bunch on Kempenfeldt Bay, Ted Justice had everyone outclassed. He was simply a wizard at the game, and when he got the ball in his possession it was as if he had it tied to his shinny with a rubber string, and it was just as hard to get it away from him as to take a bone from a bull-pup.
>
> About fifteen years ago [1905] I spent most of one afternoon riding on the front of a CPR Vancouver shunting yard engine with Teddy Justice, who had charge of those operations, and in broken-up sentences as the engine "bunked" one car here and another one somewhere else, the latter delivered something like this — "Humph! They talk about hockey teams. You betcha if we could get any of them to play a real shinny game against that old bunch that used to play on Kempenfeldt Bay with the whole bay as a rink, they'd get so sick after chasing us they'd never talk hockey anymore.

Justice's curmudgeonly views on the contemporary hockey player would probably have been even more pronounced had he lived to see the

An early hockey game on an Alberta slough, probably in the Olds area.

eventual competitive success of international hockey.

Hockey in Europe, however, was influenced by different sporting influences, not the least being soccer football, and basketball. Both of these games are based on passing and tactics. They apparently eschew rough physical contact though as anyone who has played them knows this is far from the reality. European hockey was influenced by the more subtle forms of intimidation and occasional stick work so that when North Americans played them the cries of foul were pronounced from both sides.

Europeans were repelled by the hard, physical body-checking style of their visitors, while Canadians and Americans complained of cheap shots behind the ref's back and even the clever use of feet to propel the puck (and sometimes kick rivals!). It is a long and not always pleasant difference of opinion slowly coming to an end as a universal style of play becomes supreme. Nevertheless, the wider European surface places a premium on skating and tactics in opposition to the North American use of the body.

In the process of playing Europeans, however, Canadians learned something about their own style of play and their future success. By the late 1960s and even after the somewhat pyrrhic victory of Canadian professionals over the Soviet Union in 1972, one could clearly see that unless there were major changes, the game's future belonged to Russians, Swedes, Czechs, and Finns.

Canadian ascendancy could have become a fading memory. It is a testament, therefore, to the game's hold on Canadians, that while never abandoning their physical play, they reformed their own game by improving conditioning, investing in better coaching, scouting and technology, and recognizing that skills could be taught as well as inferred.

While Canadians don't win every tournament they play today, they are almost always the favourites.

SEVEN

Climate Change: Mitigation, Resilience, and Adaptation Strategies

There is now no doubt that climate change is occurring. Even former American President George W. Bush had to finally accept that verdict. Its impact on winter and all of those items associated with the season including ice, snow, and cold have already been felt and worse appears likely to come.

In the last few years climate change has joined steroid use and inflated contracts as one of sport's troubling news stories. Athletes have collapsed and, in some cases, died in punishing summer conditions, skiing events have been cancelled in Europe because of a lack of snow, and in North America because of too much snow. Even baseball, seemingly beyond significant impact has seen its supply of bats threatened by spreading insect infestations of its timber supply.

Sports fans, athletes, and recreationists might prefer to ignore this issue, but they no longer can. It was the subject of a *Sports Illustrated* cover story in March 2007, featuring an imagined future in which Florida Marlins pitcher Dontrelle Willis is standing in water up to his knees in the team's ballpark — the anticipated result of rising sea levels.

Later that year the National Hockey League Players' Association (NHLPA) and the David Suzuki Foundation announced a partnership to promote action on climate change and environmental responsibility as they launched the "NHLPA Carbon Neutral Challenge."

By March 2009 over five hundred NHLPA members, representing all of the league's thirty teams, had signed on. Such action is notable because athletes as a community are not generally known for their progressive behaviour except when it comes to their own self-interest.

Players were encouraged to "green" their daily activities and one step was the purchase of high-quality carbon credits in recognition of the significant air travel emissions their occupation requires as they fly to cities across the North American continent from Vancouver to Florida.

The program was designed by the David Suzuki Foundation and it concluded that on average, by taking account of travel and hotel stays, each player generated ten tonnes of greenhouse gas emissions.

"It's great to see so many players showing leadership on the issue of climate change," said Dr. Suzuki. "By taking this action on global warming, these players are delivering an important message that will inspire millions of hockey fans and be a model for other sports."

One of the initiative's leaders, Andrew Ference of the Boston Bruins, applauded his fellow hockey players. "The response to the NHLPA Carbon Neutral Challenge has been amazing, especially considering we set an initial goal of encouraging seventy players to sign up. As I've said before, hockey players have great character and they continue to show it by taking action on such positive initiatives."

Hockey players grow up experiencing the joy of winter sports and very few have not spent at least some time on an outdoor rink. The variability of weather conditions over the past ten years has been some incentive for their actions, but such observation by itself can be misleading, particularly when a cold wind blows or a game is postponed because of a massive snowstorm.

Some also ridiculed the players for falling for a misleading verdict of significant global warming and suggested their naïveté reminded these critics of the players once-passionate following of hockey labour leader Alan Eagleson.

Photograph by W.B. Edwards, Library and Archives Canada PA-98952.

A hint of future global warming? This dogsled race took place in Quebec City, 1930.

Even those who applauded the players' leadership, however, recognized that it is not always easy to adequately explain the phenomenon without the eyes of observers glazing over, or a multitude of "yes, buts" being tossed out, further confusing the discussion. Though most scientists now agree the world is getting warmer, there are even a few who point to the possibility of a coming ice age.

In its most visible form, global warming is the leading factor in the revival of flora and fauna in Greenland, the disappearance of snow on Mount Kilimanjaro, the retreat of glaciers and ice fields, and the anticipated opening of the Northwest Passage whose impassable icy terrain once claimed the lives of those seeking a northern route to the Far East.

Flying home from London to Toronto in the year 2000, passengers were asked to look out the right side of the plane, and before them was the distant outline of Greenland, a white mass of land resplendent in its year-round sleep.

It had been settled by a combative Eric the Red in the tenth century and, in an early and apparent stab at the notion of truth in advertising, he selected its name as an enticement to settlement. He wasn't completely duplicitous, however, as a modest economy dependent of forests and fertile soil allowed for several hundred years of Viking crop-growing and sheep-rearing, until the Little Ice Age, beginning in the sixteenth century, put an end to even that tepid initiative.

All of that is changing. In the north, where Greenland sits above the Arctic Circle, the great ice sheet is melting. Traditional ways of life associated with this landscape are threatened, but so is the rest of the world as melting ice leads to rising sea levels and their eventual impact on coastal places.

In Greenland's south the average annual temperature from 1961 to 1990 was just above freezing at 0.5°C. By 2006 it had risen to 1.6°C. Winter is gradually arriving later in the year, and departing earlier. Crops, sheep-rearing, forestry, and boating are either possible, or soon to be, in places where they have not been before.

Global average temperature is about 0.8°C. above its level in 1750, which seems eminently manageable, except that averages don't take account of variations that are greater over different continents and even more at higher latitudes such as in Canada's north.

So one might ask, what makes this such a complex and often poorly understood issue? Is it truly a cause for worry by winter sports enthusiasts? Is it a passing aggravation? Is it an issue beholden to much larger climate changes and even fluctuations in space over which humans have little or no measurable impact? In other words, even though skeptics might acknowledge change is happening or inevitable, they argue that human action to correct it will be pointless.

Human impact on climate can also be contradictory.

Warming, a consensus of the majority of the world's scientists agree, is caused by our massive release of carbon dioxide, primarily through the combustion of fossil fuels burned mainly in industrialized countries and by deforestation mainly in developing countries.

Other releases, however, have an opposite effect.

The combustion of coal and high-sulfur fuel oil results in sulfate particulates forming in the atmosphere, which in turn bounce solar

"Spalding Ski Boots" (Made in Canada!), circa 1926.

radiation back into space. Growing concentrations of these particulates in the mid-twentieth century briefly overwhelmed the warming influence of greenhouse gas concentrations and led to a modest cooling.

These particulates, however, were implicated in the formation of acid rain with its devastating impact on lakes and general biodiversity. However, the introduction of emissions controls aimed at curtailing the creation of sulfur particulates removed a significant cooling factor in balancing the warming associated with carbon releases.

Volcanic eruptions, such as Krakatoa in 1883 and Mount Pinatubo in 1991, also created temporary periods of global cooling.

Finally the long-term and cyclical nature of climate change also plays a role, though one which humans only partially understand.

It's no accident, however, that activity like winter sports, as well as myriad other abstract activities humans engage in, from mathematical calculations to recording the meaning of their history, has happened in the relatively recent past.

We didn't suddenly become more intellectually brilliant in the last few thousand years.

The primary engine was climate stability. It was brought about by the finely tuned correspondence of heat energy received on earth and returned into space. It provided conditions for the delicate natural management of earth's temperatures within a range in which human life could not only survive, but flourish. Agriculture developed, cities grew, man went to the moon, and people competed to see who could go downhill fastest on skis.

The science, while complex, can be explained in the following way.

Carbon releases in combination with methane and nitrous oxide create what is known as the greenhouse gas effect. These gases in turn block the escape of increasing amounts of solar heat and energy. Their entrapment causes the earth's temperature to slowly rise. Alongside these effects are a build-up of water vapour–holding clouds. These add to the warming influence and additional evaporation, which results in the loss of predictable rainfall in many places. It then falls catastrophically in places where projections of its hundred-year worst-case scenario are constantly overwhelmed.

All of this might be bad enough, but as formerly solid land masses melt, they release methane gases stored in permafrost. These are even more deadly greenhouse gases, and thus accelerate, potentially beyond a range of human control, global warming.

Science has drawn a link between our carbon releases from automobiles, deforestation, coal-burning plants, and industrial production, and their impact on climate change. Some of the most significant emissions are from airplanes, hence the action of the NHLPA.

SPALDING

SPALDING SKIS

No. 84. Blue Streak Skis of specially selected seasoned hickory. Perfect in balance. Suitable for either jumping or cross-country running. Length 84 Inches..........................pair **$18.00**

No. 90. Blue Streak Skis of specially selected seasoned hickory. Perfect in balance. Suitable for either jumping or cross-country running. Length 90 inches.......................pair **$18.00**

Jumping..pair 25.00
Racing..pair 25.00

No. 72. Blue Streak Skis of specially selected seasoned ash. 72 inches...pair **$12.00**

No. 74. Blue Streak Skis of specially selected seasoned ash. 74 inches...pair **$12.00**

No. 78. Blue Streak Skis of specially selected seasoned ash. 78 inches...pair **$12.00**

No. 84. Blue Streak Skis of specially selected seasoned ash. 84 inches...pair **$12.00**

No. 90. Blue Streak Skis of specially selected seasoned ash. 90 inches...pair **$12.00**

NOTE—These skis are not supplied with harness.

No. X48. Very good quality ash, 48 inches long.........pair $2.50
No. X54. Very good quality ash, 54 inches long.........pair 3.50
No. X60. Very good quality ash, 60 inches long.........pair 4.00
No. X66. Very good quality ash, 66 inches long.........pair 4.50
No. X72. Very good quality ash, 72 inches long.........pair 5.50
No. X78. Very good quality ash, 78 inches long.........pair 7.00
No. X84. Very good quality ash, 84 inches long.........pair 8.00

NOTE—The X line of skis have rubber treads, but no harness

SPECIAL NOTE—We are unable to guarantee skis against either warping or breaking.

SKI SUNDRIES

Huitfeldt Ski Harness—Genuine Imported Norwegian.
Pair **$4.00**

Huitfeldt Harness—Canadian Made...........................pair 3.00

N. W. Norwegian Ski Harness...................................pair 2.25

Toe-straps only for Skis..pair .50

SKI WAX

Finland Wax. Packed in cans. Very essential and satisfactory.
Can **35c.**

Pocket Wax. In sticks. A great favorite for conditioning the bottoms of toboggans as well as skis. Very simple to apply.
Stick **25c.**

SKI POLES

No. 2. Ski Poles, extra heavy quality Bamboo, 6-inch ring.
Pair **$5.00**

No. 3. Ski Poles, Bamboo, extra quality.................pair 4.00

No. 4. Ski Poles of good quality Hazel wood.........pair 2.50

Rubber Sole Plates..pair .50

All prices subject to change without notice. All orders will be accepted only subject to our ability to supply the goods. Prices shown are those in effect on date noted below.

PAGE 18—JULY 5, 1926

An advertisement from the Spalding catalogue for their skis, circa 1926.

Numbers might help explain this phenomenon.

Scientists point to the concentration of carbon in the atmosphere. That number currently sits at 383 parts per million (ppm) as opposed to a recommended figure below 350 ppm. Should we reach a level of 560 ppm, many scientists believe all hope is lost and climate change will become self-reinforcing, wiping out conditions for meaningful human life. Earth will eventually recover, but by then the likelihood of human life enduring is questionable.

At the same time some have suggested we are about to leave behind the generally warm twelve-thousand-year-long Holocene period of planetary history and enter a hundred-thousand-year ice age. Winter's enthusiasts must have mixed emotions about whether they'd prefer permanent conditions in support of their sports as opposed to none.

So how does the general public make sense of this issue? One winter the ice melts early and Canadians join the doomsayers. Next year it snows every three days and we turn the other cheek to the warning of scientists. There are just enough fine points of disagreement to suggest fallacy or uncertainty in any theory.

Let's take a step back and see how we got to this point.

In the 1970s human produced carbon emissions were seen as a potentially dangerous indication of future global warming. Scientists began posting warning signals. The administration of President Ronald Reagan in Washington, D.C., not wanting to antagonize interests from the petroleum to the automotive industry for whom a business-as-usual policy had short-term profitability, reluctantly supported the establishment of the Intergovernmental Panel on Climate Change (IPCC), but not before ensuring that its research and conclusions would be constrained by criteria that eliminated from its examination and recommendations even a particle of speculation.

Nevertheless, a scientific consensus eventually emerged, unfortunately within a highly charged ideological difference of opinion, concluding that climate change was not only real, but in large measure the result of human activity.

Science, for its part, is quite cautious in jumping to these kinds of conclusions. A dominant scientific world view, such as that of Isaac

Newton, is not struck down overnight. Only when it fails to answer many questions about emerging knowledge do members of the scientific community open themselves to consideration of a more fulsome theory such as that advanced in this case by Albert Einstein, who popularized the concept of relativity.

All scientific explanations, however, are imperfect and to some degree relative because our ultimate understanding of phenomenon is a constantly improving field.

Science, which includes its testing tools and approaches, its necessity for peer review, and its confirmation of existing theories while acknowledging the possibility of disruptions in that point of view, remains our best means for understanding the world.

Skeptics may continue to argue against human activity as being significant in climate change, perhaps even as some coastal regions are drowning in rising seas and once robust winter resorts go out of business. At the end of the day it really doesn't matter. Debates are good entertainment, but they aren't science.

On the other hand a less than 1°C increase over the past century doesn't sound like much and even the worst case projections of perhaps a 5 to 6°C increase over the next century, while annoying, does not at first seem beyond human endurance. After all we can simply crank up the air conditioning in summer and, as for winter, we'll suffer through more Vancouver-type gloomy rainy winters rather than snow-shovelling ones.

The rise in the amount of snowfall in some places, and the temporary cooling in others further muddies this issue.

Climate change, however, is neither a straight line phenomenon nor necessarily intuitive. Change resulting in a warmer world will initially benefit Canada. It will extend growing seasons, open up planting possibilities in formerly hostile environments, and make Canada a tropical paradise, a wine-producing powerhouse, and a place to vacation year round.

The downside is that climate change is already destroying the livelihoods and the delicate balancing act of rival interests and cultures in many parts of Africa. A rampant extension of this catastrophe alongside a projected rise in human population from its current 6.5 billion population to perhaps as many as 9 billion by mid century may mean a world in which billions of refugees pursuing survival threaten the security of those living in gated communities at the local and national level. Geopolitical wars, famine, and disease know no boundaries.

While Canadians and other affluent westerners may in fact find snow at higher altitudes and rely on snow-making equipment at lower ones, it's hard to imagine the rest of the world allowing such carefree persons to continue with the luxury of skiing.

Canadians will have their own problems dealing with invasive species wiping out forests and urban trees and new maladies of which SARS was a precursor. Mosquitoes carrying malaria will challenge the health system's carrying capacity.

A mean temperature increase of 5°C actually indicates that the range of extreme temperatures also increases. Canadians might suddenly be confronted by the punishing possibility of temperatures and weather events, such as tornadoes and hurricanes, generally associated with the tropics. Warmer winters also could mean more days closer to those temperatures when freezing rain makes roads impassable and dependable transmission lines are brought down, as was the case of the great ice storm of 1998. It had an impact on more Canadians than any other weather event in the country's history.

Its associated impacts are already being felt in tourism, recreational fishing and hunting, insurance adjustments, forestry losses, ocean-based fisheries, adaptation expenditures, civic infrastructure, cultural fields (Canada's backyard ice rink fascination and Inuit livelihoods), and of course, the winter sports industry.

Climate change is occurring within an increasingly devastated earthly realm.

Recent studies indicate that a quarter, and the figure could be as high as 36 percent, of all land mammals and a third of those in the seas are at risk of extinction due to habitat loss and human encroachment. Climate change imposes additional stress on their habitats.

Human impact on oceans is worse than most people expected with damage including reductions in fish and sea animals as well as problems for coral reefs, seagrass beds, mangroves, rocky reefs and shelves and seamounts, and due at least in part to carbon-based acidification. Water

"Dunne's Skates: Winners Again!" from the Annual Speed Skating Meet Programme, February 9, 1929.

bodies generously capture a significant percentage of our carbon releases, but at the peril of their own health.

Invasive species are increasingly related to climate change in the form of Asian long-horned beetles wiping out urban maple tree populations, with their cooling and aesthetic function, in the American Northeast and the Mountain pine beetle now expanding beyond its devastation of the forests of British Columbia. These are forewarnings of unknown calamities we cannot even imagine.

North Americans can anticipate a reduced springtime snow pack, changing river flows, and rising sea levels affecting Vancouver, for instance, and more frequent and intense heat waves. Less severe winters will not only harm the winter sports industry, but provide an opportunity for invasive species to survive and flourish.

In Europe it means more intense winter precipitation, increasing summer heat waves and melting of mountain glaciers, a tourism shift from the Mediterranean, and intensifying regional climate differences. Its entire winter sports industry, with the exception of the highest peaks in the Alps, will be jeopardized.

The Arctic will experience significant retreat of ice, accelerated loss of ice from the Greenland ice sheet and mountain glaciers, replacement of tundra by boreal forest, and greater exposure to UV radiation. The Antarctica and Southern oceans will have an increased risk of significant ice loss from the West Antarctic Ice Sheet, thus accelerating loss of sea life. Polar bears in the Arctic and penguins in Antarctica are likely to be two species facing significant survival challenges.

The bad news is that humans are largely causing this potential catastrophe, but that's also the good news. In the immortal words of the comic strip character Pogo, we have met the enemy and he is us. So, unlike an impending meteor collision with earth that the dinosaurs could do nothing about and thus were unable to prevent their annihilation, humans can take control of our destiny. It's not a moment too soon.

We are only slowly beginning to develop some tentative responses.

LEED (Leadership in Energy and Environmental Design) is a system for rating the "green" quality of new buildings and is now incorporated in the design of many new sports facilities.

Sustainability, the Bruntland Commission's commandment of the 1980s that we should use the resources of the world wisely so as not to endanger the opportunities and comfort of future generations who will also be dependent on those resources, is an integral part of Vancouver's Winter Olympic planning, as it is for any Olympic bid that wants to be taken seriously.

The danger, however, is that greening an activity like winter sports can easily become a status quo exercise, which at best slows rather than reverses the quality of built and natural environments.

We know that even if we were to eliminate or drastically reduce all carbon emissions immediately, the impact of past practices will continue to haunt us for the rest of the century and beyond.

The National Academy of Sciences has reported that sea-level rise is inevitable as are "Dust Bowl-like" droughts persisting for at least a thousand years. They accepted as inevitable carbon dioxide concentrations of 450 ppm, eventually reaching 600 ppm if present trends continue. To put that in perspective in 1850, carbon dioxide concentrations were at 280 ppm, a level not exceeded, scientists have said, in the past eight hundred thousand years.

In the midst of all these complex responses and possibilities, the problem of winter's diminishment or disappearance seems mildly annoying, but hardly cause for hand-wringing. Yet winter's fate is directly tied to this future. Its salvation as such is embedded in the human response to climate change.

We are now starting to understand that winter's survival will have to be based on measures that go beyond conservation and maintenance to rebuilding much that has been lost or damaged. Combining restorative development with climate change resiliency provides the best opportunity for a return to the kinds of winters we have historically taken for granted.

This active engagement includes rebuilding and reconnecting the quality of natural places supporting biodiversity, adding to the stock of resilient ecosystem services including those not only supporting carbon sequestration, but also climate-change resiliency, cleaner air and water, and revitalized human-created assets from buildings to safe, diverse, and vibrant communities.

An advertisement for CCM skates from the Annual Speed Skating Meet Programme, February 9, 1929.

In other words we need to recreate conditions that Fred Grant, were he still alive, would recognize as close to those he had experienced from his own childhood in Barrie, Ontario.

Recently, however, a somewhat macabre tourism industry has grown up around visits to potentially disappearing natural phenomenon from icefields to fjords and icebergs. It was one of the latter with which an Antarctic cruise ship, *Explorer*, collided in late 2007. The iceberg survived, the boat didn't.

Visitors to these places seem aware of their contradictory behaviour — dependent on the severe greenhouse gas–emitting means of jet travel — but argue in their defense that they are actually creating new green tourist economies for local people who may be less inclined to clear cut their forests or engage in pesticide-intensive farming.

Climate change, everyone acknowledges, is complex. It's no wonder the public debate is so charged with contradictory appeals and solutions. The excesses associated with the winter sport industry are part of this dilemma. Yet if humans are adroit in their choices, there's no reason the century of climate change couldn't instead become the century of global restoration.

One team at the forefront of this changing perspective is the Buffalo Sabres hockey club. In February 2008 they announced their "Blue and Gold [the team's colours] Make Green Initiative" as part of the National Fuel Conservation Incentive Program.

The team declared their dedication "To the sustainability of the environment in Western New York and Southern Ontario.... The organization is committed to creating programming to help our fans reduce their environmental footprint and at the same time, educate Sabres fans on conservation issues, teaching fans how to be greener, and directing them to additional resources where they can learn more about environmental issues."

The Sabres' HSBC Arena manages its light use with a centrally controlled lighting system and, where appropriate, motion-sensor lighting controls. Wherever possible, fluorescent lighting is used in concourses, restrooms, and offices, and the arena's heating, ventilation, and air-conditioning system is controlled by a central building management system, with heating and cooling as necessary, based on the building's event schedule. Other operational measures included extensive recycling of all manner of products such as office paper and computer and office equipment.

Meanwhile the winter of 2009 revived one ancient tradition of hockey-playing even as its play muddied once again the climate-change discussion. For the first time in over a decade, freezing temperatures allowed members of Cambridge University's hockey team to practice on the natural ice of Bury Fen, the legendary location of early primitive forms of hockey two hundred years ago on the marshlands by the River Ouse, 120 kilometres north of London.

Then, during the first week of February, snow fell deep enough to shut London's schools, public transit, and workplaces.

Grumblers were quick to complain. This is evidence of something other than a warming trend, they said. But that's just the point scientists warned. We can expect even more climate variability of this sort in future and even the short-term promise of hockey in unexpected settings.

Be careful what you wish for, however; its long-term consequences may be severe.

EIGHT

The Meaning of Climate Change for the Future of Winter and Its Sports

The iconic symbol of the backyard ice rink, known to many of the National Hockey League players who signed on to the Climate Change Challenge, is rooted in Canadian lore and reality. The most famous belonged to Brantford's Walter Gretzky, whose boy Wayne got his start on his dad's homemade brew of packed snow and countless bitterly cold evenings of watering.

Most urbanites do not have access to a frozen pond and so like Walter Gretzky do the next best thing — they build it and the neighbourhood kids arrive.

This was the formula followed by Alfred Humber, the father and grandfather of this book's authors. An English immigrant after the Second World War, he had no heritage of rink-building. His only influence was the Harringay Racers hockey games in 1930s London.

Still he persevered. His was a narrow but deep backyard at 55 Dunfield Avenue, two blocks from Yonge and Eglinton, in the late 1950s. The backyard sloped so the surface would never meet the standards of a levelling bar and, as a result, the water ran downhill so the top part was always first to give way to grass in late winter.

Night after night he'd attach the hose to the outside water supply, having padded down the snow as best possible, and our family would hear that familiar swish of water decorating the back lawn with a fine spray. It seemed to go on for hours. He always blamed his late life rheumatism on those cold nights and no doubt there was some truth to this story.

Our job as young, not very good skaters, was to get out on the ice after school and slowly break away the jagged edges and bumps with our finely tuned stops, starts, and crossovers. The latter agility at least, is my memory, though no doubt we bore no resemblance to later kings of the backyard rink, like Brantford's "Great One."

Al Strike of Bowmanville was another "icemaster." Beginning in 1962 he handcrafted a homemade rink of old barn boards, doors, and other wooden detritus from the nearby countryside. He flooded his homemade patch long into the night, and the rink was always guaranteed at least a few more days of late winter life, owing to the great coniferous trees that ringed it on the vulnerable east, west, and south sides, his home occupying the north side.

And then in the winter of 2006–07, conditions were such that after over forty years of history the boards went up, but the ice never materialized. There weren't enough continuously cold nights to justify the late-night spraying. Fortunately, the sound of pucks slapping into Al's homemade boards late into the evening returned in 2007–08. The question remains, however, as to whether something is happening and we don't quite know what it is, other than the phenomenon of rapid climate change.

Climate change is not a straight-line cause-and-effect development. The previous chapter explored its gradual unfolding despite other accompanying and contradictory phenomenon. For instance, as noted, the climate-changing impact of human-related sulfur particles and the natural unpredictability of volcanic eruptions caused short-term global cooling. Natural climate-changing cycles lasting a millennium and longer also play a role, though it is one that is not yet fully understood.

Global warming itself will have some of its own cooling effects as melting ice at least temporarily cools surrounding territory. Most notably, some speculate that collapsing icefields and drifting colder water

Skate sailing on Grenadier Pond, High Park, Toronto, January 25, 1914.

could have an impact on the Gulf Stream, forcing it southward and away from its current role as a temperate moderator of Great Britain's climate, which, given its northerly latitude, could come to resemble that of James Bay in northern Ontario and Quebec.

The latter possibility might turn Britain into a winter sports powerhouse for at least a few years, rendering their 1936 gold medal in hockey less preposterous in future reckonings than it now appears when looking back on history.

Climate change promises fewer frozen lakes, as well. Once again in the short term this could mean more winter snow storms as evaporation from those uncovered water bodies blankets incredulous city dwellers. The ironic conclusion that many will draw is that global warming is a chimera, and policies and programs in support of its mitigation, or strategies supporting human adaptability and more resilient built and natural environments, are unnecessary luxuries.

The longer-term perspective, however, is the only one that counts when it comes to climate change, though this long term can be counted in the decades rather than millennia. Even here the loss of our winter heritage might strike few as being cause for anything other than nostalgic concern.

Warmer weather will simply usher in other activities. Perhaps, like buggy-whip manufacturers and typewriter-repair people, we should merely lament their passing as an inevitable result of progress. Except, of course, this has nothing to do with progress.

Urbanization and the increasing affluence of city residents allowed winter sports to evolve from a recreation into a commodity, even if it was one increasingly restricted to a higher-earning clientele. Critics might suggest we shouldn't bemoan the potential loss of such an industry. No era, however, can afford to be cavalier about the failure of its successful economic engines, particularly if its other parts are in crisis.

On the other hand, winter sports are not innocent bystanders to the factors threatening their survival. Snow-making equipment, for instance, is energy- and water-intensive, while the attraction of faraway prestigious resorts requires considerable air travel. Closer to home, ski resorts and weekend hockey tournaments usually necessitate significant automotive commuting. There are few better "canary in the coal mine" reference points for climate change's impact.

At the fifth World Conference on Sport and Environment held in the then future Winter Olympics site of Turin, Italy, in 2003, three scholars, Rolf Burki, Hans Elsasser, and Bruno Abegg examined the environmental and economic consequences of climate change and winter sports.

"Mountain areas," they said, "are sensitive to climate change. Implications of climate change can be seen ... in less snow, receding glaciers, melting permafrost, and more extreme events like landslides." The ultimate result would be a ski industry climbing the mountains, as it were, to reach snow-reliable areas at higher altitudes, with resulting impact on the economy of lower altitude communities dependent on the sport.

As well, the melting of permafrost not only leaves these mountain areas vulnerable to landslides, and in the summer, rockfalls, but threatens the bracing and anchoring of cableway stations, lift masts, and buildings. As mentioned in the previous chapter, melting permafrost releases even higher quantities of greenhouse gases, thus exacerbating the climate-change impact and contributing to the real possibility of runaway change beyond the mediating capacity of human action.

Nor do we have to await the full impact of climate change. Economic self-sufficiency for resorts and local tourist economies in the European Alps, dependent on winter sports, generally requires a snow reliability of at least seven of ten winters with coverage of thirty to fifty centimetres on at least one hundred days between December 1 and April 15. While in 2003, 85 percent of Switzerland's 230 ski resorts were in that range, the number could fall to 63 percent by mid century.

Climate change would have an even more severe impact in Germany and Austria where resorts are at a lower altitude. Likewise, in Australia the worst-case scenario would effectively banish the sport to only the highest altitudes and its dependence on expensive snow-making resources. Canadian and American resorts, with existing investment in such equipment, might be less harshly hit, though it's difficult to predict whether their energy and water demands might become prohibitive.

Possibly the greatest long-term impact would be the availability of financing for costly retrofits of ski operations. Even before the financial meltdown of 2008, banks were only prepared to provide limited and very restrictive loans to ski resorts at altitudes below 1500 metres, causing some to wonder if such places should simply be abandoned to find another purpose. They have not been shut down as yet, often for good regional economic reasons, but their future is hardly encouraging even with the shift in some cases to indoor skiing.

In 2007, one desperate ski-lift company in Ernen, Switzerland, sold its four ski lifts, two trail groomers, and a restaurant on twelve miles of ski slopes to a British entrepreneur for about one American dollar. They were unable to bear annual losses of $180,000 and the obligation to renew their $1.4 million operating license.

A Canadian government report, "From Impacts to Adaptation: Canada in a Changing Climate 2007," documented a 10 percent decrease in snow cover in the northern hemisphere for the period 1972–2003, with a decrease of twenty days duration of snow cover in the Arctic since 1950, a cautionary note for those who think that winter sports activity would simply move north if it disappeared from the affluent south.

The authors note the impact of climate change on cultural identity. This includes the tenuous connection of urban-dwelling Canadians to the seasons, kept alive in winter by backyard rinks and weekend ski trips. During a conference call in mid November 2006 with a community college representative in Iqaluit, those in an Ottawa hotel room discussing energy-management solutions to climate change impact were startled by her comment that people in Nunavut were still fishing on open waters, "And that," she said, "is insane for this time of year." One can only imagine what this means in the longer term for the cultural identity and livelihood of Inuit peoples.

Nor is the impact the same everywhere. Ironically, climate change may result in more snow in some regions. While precipitation has declined in most of southern Canada in the last half century, lake-effect snow has actually increased in the western part of southern Ontario; a factor potentially related to evaporation off open, as opposed to frozen, water bodies — another climate-change impact.

In 2006, a long-term study by Vincent and Mekis for the period of 1950 to 2003, observed the following climatic conditions generally occurring throughout Canada. They included fewer extreme cold nights, fewer extreme cold days, and fewer frost days, not that this would garner many complaints from those who have to start their car or walk to work on such days.

They further noted that there had been a decrease in annual total snowfall in southern Canada, and an increase in annual total snowfall in northern and northeastern Canada.

The impact of the first three factors has immediate meaning for backyard-rink builders with the exception of a new breed using artificial means. Affluent Canadians unwilling to accept limitations on their outdoor hockey tradition have resorted to expensive energy-and-water-intensive solutions.

Up-market backyard rinks consisting of stadium lighting, mini Zambonis, full boards, and actual refrigeration systems are now available. Average customized rinks can cost $75,000 while those of NHL standards might run to a million dollars. This way the outdoor season can run from November through March. Former Toronto Maple Leaf Wendel Clark's thirty-eight-metre rink north of Toronto was profiled in the *Globe and Mail* in 2008. Nor was he alone, as other former players and wealthy Torontonians have entered this specialized market.

The Toronto Girl:
"Tobogganing"

"The Toronto Girl: 'Tobogganing.'"

Warming, however, is expected to be greatest in the winter months due partly, experts say, to the feedback effect that reduced snow and ice cover has on land-to-surface albedo. In simple terms, white surfaces reflect light and associated heat, whereas darker surfaces absorb it, rendering even expensive artificial ice-making options, such as the above, fruitless at a certain point.

Throughout the country, climate change would provide both benefits and challenges. While the length of the skiing season would decline in southern regions of Quebec, including Montreal and the Eastern Townships, less harsh conditions in January and February would increase the attractiveness of downhill skiing and the use of trails for other sports. Latitude and altitude would benefit the bigger ski resorts of Mont Tremblant, Mont-Sainte-Anne, and Le Massif. On the other hand, winter carnivals and the sport of ice fishing might be more vulnerable to unpredictable conditions.

In the winter of 2005–06, ice fishing disappeared from Lake Erie near Buffalo and with it the greater spending that ice fishermen contributed to local communities as opposed to that of summertime anglers.

The compression of the winter season also narrows the window of opportunity for those remaining winter sports that are dependent on outside conditions. Projections of a 50-percent shorter winter in Ontario and snow-cover reductions, in that limited period, of up to 35 percent are considered likely. The Christmas period of 2006 was particularly problematic for Ontario's Blue Mountain resort, which closed down its skiing and snowboarding operations in mid December while golf courses opened in Durham Region on Christmas Day. At what point do activities like snowmobiling and cross-country skiing become irrelevant?

The south shore of Georgian Bay is a prime downhill-skiing destination with variable projections into the 2020s ranging from no seasonal reduction to as high as 16 percent. Large operators have diversified real estate and four-season activities, as well as snow-making equipment, allowing them to manage at least in the immediate future, any significant adjustment in snowfall and unpredictable weather.

In western Canada the impact varies though generally higher altitude ski locations in Banff and environs would feel minimal impact. At lower altitudes, however, snow-making becomes essential and certain activities like snowshoeing, cross-country skiing, and snowmobiling, requiring extensive, rather than intensive, land coverage, would be vulnerable. Areas like the Whistler-Blackcomb site of the 2010 Winter Olympics have diversified themselves to withstand any short-term impact.

The survival instinct of winter sport enthusiasts, however, should not be underestimated. In the Netherlands the "Journey of Eleven Cities" or *Elfstedentocht*, is an occasional event held on the canals and lakes around Leeuwarden, a city of ninety thousand in the region of Friesland. Only fifteen races were held in the twentieth century with the first held in 1909 and projections for the twenty-first century are for no more than four.

Unfortunately, the event obviously depends on freezing temperatures, and therefore it hasn't been held since 1997. That year a blocking low-pressure system centred over Scandinavia allowed cold air from Russia to drive down temperatures.

Nor is the event's future promising as the winter of 2005–06 was the warmest since records had been kept in 1706. Yet anticipation remains high that a magic year will return as it did in the southern part of the Netherlands in early 2009 as once again a blocking weather pattern brought freezing conditions. Skaters returned to the Dutch countryside and casualties included the country's minister of defence who, perhaps not used to such conditions, tumbled on the ice, resulting in several broken bones. Meanwhile, others have taken up roller skating, bicycle races, and even solar-driven boats so that an annual competition can proceed without dependence on winter conditions.

Are there any measures that might ensure winter's survival?

Possibly, but almost assuredly not in all of the places where it is now taken for granted.

Mitigation and adaptation measures may provide a stopgap hope and a turning-point opportunity so that not just the memory of winter, but little pockets of its expression will survive as harbingers of a restored balance.

These pockets, be they higher-altitude ski resorts, or artificially refrigerated backyard rinks, may have to be the foundation for a rebirth,

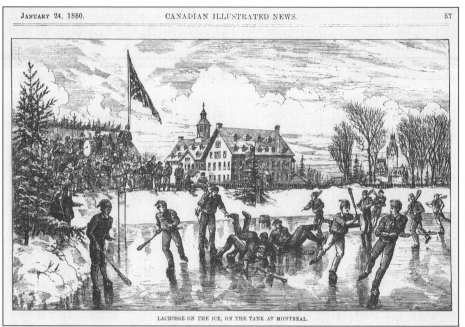

Lacrosse on ice in Montreal — a precursor of these athletes' switch to hockey, from the Canadian Illustrated News, *January 24, 1880.*

or, like the occasional skating race of the Netherlands, a suggestion of what could be.

The challenge for organizers of the 2010 Vancouver Winter Olympics then was to stage an event that did not contribute to the destruction of what is being celebrated.

It was almost an impossible task. Human activity and steps to reduce its impact often result in unexpected additional harm. Even wind turbines, the new poster child for environmentally friendly energy production, require energy to build, transport, mount, and maintain; offend the aesthetic sensibilities of many living nearby (the same people, of course, who would scream if their electrical supply was cut off); necessitate, in many cases, long transmission lines to deliver the energy captured; and, because of wind's indeterminate regularity, must be supplemented by other energy sources, which in some cases are plants whose energy is captured from coal.

"Sustainability," said Ann Duffy, the Vancouver Organizing Committee's corporate sustainability officer, in the event's sustainability report, "is a mindset. It's about planning for the future and thinking about long-term impacts, locally and globally."

The criticism of sustainability, however, is that its measurement can be a slippery slope — sustainable for how long, and for whom, and under what conditions?

In any case, the Olympic organizers have shown their willingness to try, and, in the process possibly define the concept in more rigorous terms. They are consciously addressing their impact in terms of:

- Location and size of land used within or near protected areas or areas of high biodiversity value.
- Number of infractions and/or value of monetary fines for non-compliance with environmental laws and regulations.
- Number and volume of significant spills.
- Total energy consumed.
- Total greenhouse gas (GHG) emissions.
- Composition of vehicle fleet: total number; percent with low-emission features.
- Number of newly constructed venues and/or villages applying for independent certification under the Leadership in Energy and Environmental Design (LEED) green building rating system.
- Weight of waste diverted from landfill and percent of total.

These admirable performance measurements were matched by some significant actions.

When twelve plant species were found in a small wetland intended as the site for a future snow-making reservoir, they were moved, sometimes by hand, to a site similar in character to the original.

The Whistler Sliding Centre for bobsled, luge, and skeleton events required the refrigeration of what is essentially a long outdoor exposed surface — kind of like leaving your doors and windows open in the winter and then turning on the air conditioning to compensate for any small difference in temperature.

According to David Sinclair of Cimco Refrigeration, the company responsible for this project, "Sliding guys are even more finicky in ice-making than those who prepare indoor surfaces for curling."

Something like fifty-two thousand staff hours were required to prepare the venue's refrigeration, not surprising given that it contains a 228-metre elevation change from top to bottom, in which even tiny changes in microclimate could be devastating. Engineers were aware of what happened at the ski jump slide in the 2002 Salt Lake City Winter Games, when a warming front made it difficult to maintain snow at the bottom of the slide.

Nothing can be left to chance, which of course is part of the sustainability challenge. In a world that truly believed in sustainability we would accept that everything might not meet our needs and so be content with waiting. The Olympics, however, are a time-certain and televised event. They have a low tolerance for delay or the unexpected. Over-engineering might be good for higher assurance, but it can be destructive for wider environmental respect.

The Whistler-Blackcomb venue construction was rushed due to delays and rain, but it resulted in some on-site erosion, which included surface soil instability and sedimentation. Organizers acknowledged the error of their ways and amended their procedures. In an increasingly financially constrained world and at the time of actually staging winter events, such caution might no longer be possible.

Likewise, major upgrades to the Sea to Sky Highway from Vancouver to Whistler required the removal of pristine forest along with mountainside blasting to allow for road widening. It's an old truism, however, that traffic expands to fill the space allotted for it and this route will be no exception. More traffic will ultimately mean more emissions.

As well, the brilliant, highly visible, and television-friendly orange Olympic flame is the product of a butane and propane mixture that produces unacceptable levels of greenhouse gas emissions. As a result, for the torch relay, plans were to replace it with a more efficient and environmentally benign substitute. It sounded good in theory, but it was a flame that could barely be seen. "If you can't see it," a torch relay spokesperson said, "what's the point?"

A careful consideration of the challenges facing organizers is three-fold. Whatever they do they will contribute to the very factors likely

A horse race on the Ottawa River, March 1902.

to either erase or make less likely a world of dramatic winter weather. Secondly, even the best choices are often creating a new sustainable resource at the expense of another. And finally, even environmental proponents can do harm by focusing on a "nickel and dime" recitation of incremental damage while losing sight of the larger agenda.

The last point is significant. Environmental critics have been quick for instance to condemn persons whose idle Googling of frivolous web sites creates at least some limited demand on energy sources. The problem with such a criticism is that not only is frivolity one of the main reasons for Googling, but that such activity may keep people from engaging in more environmentally destructive activities.

Likewise, criticizing the Olympics because they are not impact-free and absolutely carbon neutral and sustainable is beside the point. The Olympics are the ultimate expression of human frivolousness. We care about someone going down a hill faster than someone else. What could be more pointless than that? We care whether our men's and women's hockey teams win gold. Can anything be more frivolous? Perhaps it is to Americans, but not to Canadians.

In this case its frivolousness is its cultural beauty. It's what makes us human.

The most important legacy of the Vancouver Winter Olympics isn't their perfection but their willingness, as most recent Olympic events have been prepared to do, to consciously address their environmental footprint.

Unfortunately, our responses are still rooted in the idea that we have to tear down what already exists to create something that is "greener."

Possibly the most environmentally pure Olympics ever held were the Summer Games in London, England, in 1948. Britain had no money to build fancy new settings or even the resources to significantly improve existing facilities, so they had to make do with what they had. Unfortunately it has earned the tag as the "Austerity Games," a branding suggesting its lowbrow and cheap quality.

What if one were to mount Games based solely on the notion of making use of what was already in place and then channeling extra dollars into either upgrading functionally acceptable locations or restoring the life of degraded ones? These would be a true Olympics for a new era of restorative development.

More to the point, they would ensure that any interest in greening winter events or making them more sustainable is directly measurable by virtue of what is either returned to life or what is enhanced for better long-term performance.

Finally, one must address the necessity of the Games themselves. Can we afford frivolity in economically depressed times? Should we support even the best intentions of organizers on the environmental front when we know that ultimately this exercise will simply slow the rate of destruction rather than reversing it?

Even Vancouver organizers have understood this dilemma.

Venue construction and vehicle use increased 67 percent in one year through the spring of 2008, resulting in a greenhouse-gas production that can only be offset by purchasing carbon credits in the form of tree-planting or energy efficiency measures elsewhere, or installing renewable energy capture. As it has been noted, the latter is problematic.

Critics have further pointed out that while local timber was used in constructing the new speed-skating facility in Richmond, it had problems with mould and parts needed to be replaced. After the Games, the site will be reconfigured for other purposes, resulting in further energy and construction impact.

Likewise, the soapstone souvenirs of green serpents have increased demand and energy-intensive quarrying for this difficult-to-extract resource. And while hydrogen-fuelled buses will operate throughout the Games, the fuel used for other related Olympic travel, whether by spectators or for shipping products and competitors, will depend on traditional carbon-spewing means.

The criticisms will never end, but the beauty of the Games is their inspirational character and the slow rise to realizing the need to address environmental impact, and associated social, economic, and First Nations issues and participation.

The appropriate response goes beyond reducing environmental impact. It requires the deliberate addition to our stock of built and natural assets by meeting the challenge of human habitability — how we live, where we live, and what we do in the places we live. The Winter Olympics are neither the solution nor the problem, but they're not a bad place to begin asking substantive questions.

So there's no need for Canadians to feel guilty about celebrating the Winter Olympics in their country or for cheering on the home team as it mounts the podium to receive gold, silver, or bronze recognition. Engaging in such activity is part of the magnificence of human living.

The experience of human joy reminds us that improvement is possible and desirable. Our engagement in the Olympic exercise provides clues as to the ways we might address not only the sustainability of winter sports, but the larger question of how we restore our world. If we cannot solve the climate-change challenge, it is certain these will be the last Winter Olympics held in Canada because there will not be guaranteed winter conditions to ensure their continuance.

One last possibility, of course, is taking the entire event indoors, but then we will be certain that the splendid sporting season will have lost its relevance and that would be a significant tragedy. It would not only be admitting defeat, but continuing the downward slide of human connivance in environmental destruction, which has got us to where we are now and for which too many of our solutions remain stopgap measures.

No one wants to be the aging grandparent who, on his or her deathbed, has to tell a grandchild that warm, snow-free winter days and punishing summers are the price we paid for a temporary assault on the world's cherished splendour.

Meanwhile, Al Strike's homemade front-lawn ice rink was attracting neighbourhood children by the first weeks of January 2009 and the annual "world" ball-hockey-on-ice event went ahead as scheduled at the end of the month. Just as well! Within two weeks, mild weather had reduced the rink to patches of ice and grass.

Regular snow on a three-day cycle and deep-freeze temperatures had guaranteed another reminder of winter's glories, but for how long one can never be sure.

NINE

The Romance of Winter Sports: Will It Eventually Go Indoors?

What could the Winter Olympics look like in forty years, if the earth's temperature continues to rise, and winters in typically cold climates become more unpredictable? Could we see Winter Olympic officials embracing more snow-producing machines, providing athletes with a solely man-made environment for competition? Could the Games simply be moved farther and farther north with, if necessary, snow being imported, as organizers did for the 1932 Winter Olympics in Lake Placid? Perhaps the entire Games will simply be moved indoors? Or maybe, more alarmingly, there simply won't be a Winter Olympics in forty years.

There are many avenues that future Winter Olympics could explore. Unquestionably, the Games generate significant global interest, and many countries, despite these climate concerns, would still want to compete. If there is a significantly altered climate in the future, so that fewer countries have acceptable outdoor conditions for holding events, Olympic organizers will have to adapt. The main change will ultimately be the hosting city's facilities.

Warning signs have already been issued by reputable groups like The World Resources Institute (WRI). In a press conference in Salt Lake City in 2002, Jonathan Lash, president of WRI, expressed a dire plea: "Global Warming threatens future Winter Olympic Games because it is resulting in less snow, and shorter and warmer winters."

Four years later, in Turin, American environmental activist Laurie David expressed similar concerns, posting her thoughts on the future of the Winter Games in the *Huffington Post*. "It's been unseasonably warm in Turin, something that is readily apparent in all those sweeping shots of 'no' [as opposed to snow]-covered Alps the TV cameras keep showing us.

"Watching Matt Lauer conduct interviews outside the Olympic Stadium clad in little more than a light sweater — no jacket, no gloves, no scarf — I can't help but feel a preemptive pang of nostalgia for a global tradition sadly marked for extinction."

The alpine region is of significant concern, with rapidly melting glaciers (where the best snow is usually found), climate scientists have warned that possibly half of all the glaciers in the world could be gone within the next one hundred years.

It makes one wonder how many countries could conceivably host the Winter Olympics in future years. It's a contentious issue to be certain, as the Olympics receive bids from countries across the globe. Simply moving all future Winter Olympics to a neutral site, located in the region of the North Pole, for example, where facilities would be constructed and used every four years might simply usher in the beginning death knell of the Games. A new host city of the Winter Games every four years adds to its appeal by offering a fresh new backdrop for the Olympic experience, and a unique identifier in the history books.

The warming of the global climate also affects the training of a country's athletes. Problems have arisen already with athletes seeking guaranteed facilities in which to develop skills necessary to produce winning results in Winter Olympic events. If winter is affected by prolonged, warmer summers, and shortened winters, countries that traditionally have produced dozens of Olympic-calibre athletes may find their outdoor facilities aren't available even in normal winter months. Their athletes simply won't be at the same level as

Skating and hockey go indoors at the Victoria Skating Rink. "Race Between Young Girls" from the Canadian Illustrated News, *March 23, 1872.*

competitors from countries that have had typically harsh winters in the past, or countries that have developed expensive environmentally questionable indoor facilities. With no intervention or plan in place to counteract this possible situation, the Winter Games could eventually involve only the richest countries that have created faux environments for training purposes. On the other hand, something of this sort is already developing.

Or, more facetiously, the Olympics could go the way envisioned by an *Atlanta Journal-Constitution* writer: "By 2014, there might not be enough snow and ice left on the planet; the Winter Games may become the Water Games. So curling will go the way of chariot races, and the Norwegians, the Finns and the Lithuanians will have to play basketball."

It seems most likely that the future of the Winter Olympics will rely on a trend that has already developed — adapting to a changing climate by shielding oneself from it. With snow becoming more sparse and hard to come by, indoor facilities are now being built. Retractable roofs have become commonplace in stadiums across North America to accommodate fans and athletes in reaction to unpredictable weather conditions, and the idea is catching on with other countries in making impressive indoor facilities that can host sports that are not typically thought of as being indoor games.

Take, for example, Finland's indoor cross-country training centre. It offers indoor cross-country skiing and biathlon opportunities year-round in a tunnel. Skiing indoors does not have the same atmosphere as one would get while skiing outside amidst open sky and surrounding mountains, with animals and real trees in the distance. It does, however, offer the same benefits that domed stadiums do, namely the ability to create an artificial indoor world where the temperature can be controlled and snow will not disappear based on a natural warm front, and where, ironically, one can train when it is too cold outdoors.

The idea of the training centre was conceived in the 1980s when Finland acknowledged that their skiers need to train year-round. The developers of the centre and facilities like the Torsby Ski Tunnel in Sweden were reacting to a realization that skiers who wanted to train in the summer had some significant difficulties. In order for the skiers to find

Curling in an unheated, but indoor, barn in 1914. From left to right: Reverend J.W. McMillan, Reverend J.C. Walker, Reverend C.W. Gordon, and Reverend C. McKinnon.

ideal snow, they were forced to train up in mountains where the altitude was so high that it hindered their abilities, and was difficult to reach. The solution was to build an indoor tunnel where skiers could replicate the outdoor activities in a climate-controlled, indoor-skiing wonderland, and in which snow could be made when it was up to 25°C outside.

Developers witnessed snow-making in laboratory conditions and knew that it was feasible. They put shovels in the ground and started construction in April 1997. In just eight short months, the tunnel was completed. There were a few difficulties in the early stages as they discovered that on humid, rainy summer days, the snow in the tunnel would become wet and slow. Reacting to this, the developers installed dryers on the roof and inside the tunnel. This worked, as within the next few days, humidity decreased by 20 percent.

The tunnel proved a success, as today it is used exclusively for skiing,

Author's collection.

Wilfrid "Blondy" Sutcliffe, captain and defenceman for the Goodyear Tire and Rubber Company Senior Ontario Hockey Association team, circa 1934.

though on some days, when the outside weather co-operates, curling is also possible.

This facility is far from the only new innovative building that has brought traditional outdoor winter sports to the indoors. While creating a facility that can accommodate cross-country skiing indoors is an impressive feat, creating a facility that can accommodate indoor ski jumping was a bigger challenge.

Dubai is host of some of the most awe-inspiring pieces of architecture in the world, but perhaps none are more impressive than Ski Dubai, which is an unbelievable structure that is over twenty thousand square metres and covered with snow throughout the year. The facility is complete with five different ski jumps that range in difficulty from beginner to those that challenge even the best ski jumpers in the world.

The remarkable facilities feature climate-controlled temperatures that keep the snow from melting, and also keep the customers who use the facilities comfortable, as well. It's a little Utopia of ski jumping without setting foot outdoors.

Less successful than Ski Dubai's indoor ski jump was Japan's indoor ski jump LaLaport Skidome, which was given the acronym SSAWS (Spring Summer Autumn Winter Snow). The slope opened in the early 1990s amidst considerable intrigue over being the first-ever indoor ski-jump facility.

Weighing in at a cost of nearly a half a billion dollars, the hope was the facility would be able to break even by 2018. However, due to unforeseen economic troubles in Japan, revenue was much lower than expected, and the operating costs ended up being more than the annual returns for the facility. SSAWS closed in 2002 and it was demolished in 2003, making way for an IKEA store on the site.

Ironically, these indoor facilities may themselves add to the environmental crisis the world currently faces. Their energy demands are direct contributors to global warming. One of these controversial indoor winter facilities is SnOasis, currently in development in England.

SnOasis is an ambitious project that has joined the trend of bringing winter sports indoors. The resort will include a massive indoor ski slope that would challenge Dubai's biggest jump at 415 metres long with a hundred-metre vertical drop that meets Olympic standards.

A hockey club in Trail, British Columbia, 1914.

Along with this massive ski jump, the resort also features smaller ski slopes, a bobsled track and luge run, an outdoor ice rink, cross-country skiing, a speed-skating track, and an ice-climbing wall. They also intend to add non-winter facilities to complement this winter sports fantasy world, with tennis courts, windsurfing, sailing, and fishing, amongst the other available sports.

Critics argue that SnOasis could generate at least thirty-four thousand tons of CO_2 emissions a year, and so add to the very causes of further climate change that made such a facility necessary in the first place. Its developers have insisted that most of their energy will come from renewable sources, and they plan to plant over one hundred thousand trees to act as a carbon sink, but this has done little to calm protesters who have responded by saying that the new woodland would in no way counteract the amount of emissions produced.

The concern over the development and use of facilities for future cities hoping to host the Olympics has been addressed by the United Nations Environment Program (UNEP), who believe that the best course of action for the candidate cities is to abandon events in the mountain areas.

While many casual fans wondered why the Turin Olympics in 2006 didn't make more use of the mountains, UNEP said that, "Contrary to some suggestions that the Winter Olympics were held too far from the mountains, Turin may in fact have shown the way toward even more environmentally friendly Winter Olympics." They praised Turin Olympic developers for not putting too much wear and tear on the delicate mountain environment.

Turin was not without criticism, though, as the bobsled track built in the mountains was criticized by UNEP, who said in their report, "Constructing, operating and maintaining what is effectively a huge fridge in the mountains raises many fundamental questions of sustainability." It's a huge fridge with its doors left opened as it were, and one that is directly exposed to the outdoor elements.

Reusing and updating existing facilities was one of the main suggestions of UNEP chief Klaus Toepfer.

An unpredictable future, and how climate change will affect different countries, has lead to some outlandish suggestions from those who believe that eventually their location may become one of the few places best able to hold the Games.

Web developers of the site *www.winterolympics2026.com* argue that the west of Ireland is heading for a mini ice age in the near future. They suggest that Ireland might be a perfect spot for a Winter Games in 2026.

The site quotes from an article from the *Irish Independent*, June 21, 2001: "Ireland's winter climate could become as cold as Moscow's. New evidence has raised fears that the warm Gulf Stream which dominates the Irish climate is beginning to lose its impact. It would mean that a warmer world caused by the man-made emissions of greenhouse gases could paradoxically lead to a colder and more uncomfortable climate for Ireland."

The site tells its viewers to "Be Prepared!"

Despite the peculiar hope of some that a modest ice age will envelop Ireland, it could all be for naught. The Winter Olympics walk a tightrope in considering what events and facilities have the best environmental and practical future. They appear to be favouring the idea of bringing the Games indoors, and creating additional climate-controlled buildings.

A map of Montreal from Baedeker's Canada travel guide in 1900; note the number of skating rinks.

Vancouver is showcasing this new era of the Winter Games by its use, for the first time in either summer or winter Olympic history, of an indoor domed stadium — BC Place.

In another sign of future choices, Vancouver, having an average temperature of 4.8°C (40.6°F), is the warmest city ever to host the Winter Games.

The development of facilities for the Winter Olympics in 2014, hosted by Sochi, Russia, is being watched by critical environmental eyes. Vladimir Putin promised facilities that will put less strain on the earth.

In July 2008, he ordered organizers to relocate some of their planned locations, including the bobsled track, and Olympic village, in response to environmental concerns by groups like Greenpeace and the World Wildlife Fund. They warned that the proposed construction sites for these amenities were simply too close to wilderness areas.

Despite concerns over the impracticality of having new sites ready for the Games, and cost concerns, Putin's order was clear, "In setting our priorities and choosing between money and the environment, we're choosing the environment."

Putin further explained his decision: "If the balance of nature is upset, this could lead to a situation that would be impossible to restore for any amount of money."

The statement thrilled environmentalists who declared nature as being the first victors in the 2014 Olympic Games. It also added tension between environmentalists and facility developers. They said Putin's concern over the environment, and his declaration that changes needed to be made, could possibly add up to another six months of preparations, and additional costs, as Russia's planned $12 billion budget would easily be surpassed. Some officials believed the cost could double.

The Vancouver Games have also reacted to mounting pressure from environmentalists by producing reports on how their facilities are being developed in relation to their impact on Vancouver's terrain. Officials have produced documentation showing that many of their sites selected came from a federal environment assessment review process.

In the years ahead there will be more of this kind of tug-of-war between environmentalists and developers. Environmentalists argue that while creating environmentally sound facilities may initially cost more, creating environmentally damaging amenities is much more financially damaging to a city in the long run.

What will the future Olympics look like? If the Winter Olympics are to continue, it appears that in reaction to the warming climate, it is unlikely that the Games will retreat farther north to accommodate the

A speed skating poster from Taylor's Arena in Bowmanville, Ontario.

globally changing landscape. Instead, as in Vancouver, they will have to adjust the ways they react to the unpredictability of climate.

In the future, whether we like it or not, the Olympics will depend on more artificial indoor environments.

In time, it's conceivable that the Winter Olympics could open the doors to any city willing to spend the necessary dollars to host them, and ignore the fact that such a city may not have a winter season. A Winter Olympics in the desert? Sounds implausible, but the day may come when the Winter Olympics might become simply the Indoor Olympics, and Canadians looking to recall those days of snow and ice and winter frost will have to visit a climate-controlled entertainment emporium for a last reminder of what once defined them.

Is that too dreary a picture? One hopes not, but the challenges are before us. Our response and commitment to preserving and restoring the very thing that has helped define us will be Canada's story for the twenty-first century.

NOTES AND SOURCES

Chapter One

Fred W. Grant's memories of his boyhood in 1880s Barrie, Ontario, entitled "Boyhood's Popular Winter Pastimes in Barrie Over Forty years Ago," appeared in the *Barrie Examiner* in 1921 and are today stored in the Simcoe County Archives. For the story of early skating on the slough, Ardrossan Women of Unifarm, *Cherished Memories* (Ardrossan, Alberta: c.1972), 534. The year Lake Ontario froze solid appeared in Adam Mayers, "When Winter Was Cool," *Toronto Star*, February 8, 2007, R4. The evolution of the modern city is described in Gunther Barth's *City People: The Rise of Modern City Culture in Nineteenth-Century America* (New York: Oxford University Press, 1980); Douglas Rae, *City: Urbanism and Its End* (New Haven: Yale University Press, 2003).

Chapter Two

Sources included Eugene Benson and William Toye, *The Oxford Companion to Canadian Literature* 2nd ed. (Toronto: Oxford

University Press, 1997); John Robert Colombo, *The Dictionary of Canadian Quotations* (Toronto: Stoddart, 1991); Roy McGregor, *Canadians: A Portrait of a Country and Its People* (Toronto: Penguin Books, 2007); Geoff Pevere and Greig Dymond, *Mondo Canuck: A Canadian Pop Culture Odyssey* (Scarborough: Prentice Hall, 1996). Viewing of Canadian Broadcasting Corporation shows featuring Rick Mercer; American television shows featuring Conan O'Brien; and pop cultural sources contributed to this chapter's insights.

Chapter Three

The *New York Clipper*, one of the leading sports and entertainment journals of the nineteenth century, was consulted for its commentary on winter sports in Canada. For information on snowshoeing, see William Humber, "Taking Snow in Their Stride," *Horizon Canada*, Vol. 9, No. 99 (1987): 2366; Hugh Becket, *The Montreal Snow Shoe Club: Its History and Record with a Synopsis of Racing Events of Other Clubs Through the Dominion from 1840 to the Present Time* (Montreal: 1882).

Chapter Four

Various official sports web sites were consulted for general background information, as well the quoted memories of Fred W. Grant. General Canadian sports histories were referenced, including S.F. Wise and Douglas Fisher, *Canada's Sporting Heroes* (Don Mills, ON: General Publishing, 1974); Howell and Howell, *Sports and Games in Canadian Life* (Toronto: Macmillan, 1974); Alannah Hegedus and Kaitlin Rainey, *Shooting Hoops and Skating Loops: Great Inventions in Sports* (Toronto: Tundra, 1999); Colin Howell, *Blood, Sweat, and Cheers: Sport and the Making of Modern Canada* (Toronto, University of Toronto Press: 2001). Specific sports were researched, including, John A. Stevenson, *Curling in Ontario: 1846–1946* (Toronto: Ontario Curling Association, 1950); Christopher Ondaatje and Gordon Currie, *Olympic Victory* (Winnipeg: Greywood, n.d.); Edwin C. Guillet, *Early Life in Upper Canada* (Toronto: University of Toronto Press, 1933).

Chapter Five

Olympic source material included background writings of Martin Harris on the 1936 Olympic hockey tournament and clippings from the English papers of the day, including the *Evening News*, the *Daily Telegraph*, the *Daily Sketch*, the *Daily Mail*, the *Guardian*, and the *Times*. Barbara Ann Scott's story is featured in a variety of sources including, Barbara Ann Scott, *Skate With Me*, (Garden City, NY: Doubleday, 1950): and Cay Moore, *She Skated into Our Hearts* (Toronto: McClelland and Stewart, 1948). Other texts include Bob Ferguson, *Who's Who in Canadian Sport* (Markham, ON: Fitzhenry and Whiteside, 2005). As well, texts cited in Chapter Four, such as Wise and Fisher, and Howell and Howell, were also of assistance.

Chapter Six

Background on origins is available from Society for International Hockey Research (SIHR), "The Origins of Hockey" (May 2002); William Houston, "Nova Scotia: Hockey's Birthplace," *Globe and Mail*, November 15, 1996; J.W. (Bill) Fitsell, *How Hockey Happened* (Kingston: Quarry Books, 2006); Randy Boswell, "U.S. History Takes shots at Canada's Game," *National Post*, December 31, 2008, 2. The *Toronto Globe* and the *Toronto Star* from the 1880s and 1890s provided numerous accounts of hockey incidents, as well as the words of Fred. W. Grant.

Chapter Seven

Sources included: D.S. Lemmen, F.J. Warren, J. Lacroix, E. Bush, eds., "From Impacts to Adaptation: Canada in a Changing Climate 2007" (Ottawa: Government of Canada, 2008); National Geographic, "Changing Climate" (Washington: National Geographic Society, 2008); The Geo-4 Global Environment Outlook, "Summary for Decision Makers" (United Nations Environment Programme, 2007); "Climate Change," *Geographical Magazine*, Vol. 80, No.10 (October 2008); "Global Warming Skepticism," *Skeptic Magazine*, Vol. 14, No. 1 (2008); Intergovernmental Panel on Climate Change (IPCC), "Climate Change 2007: Impacts, Adaptation and

Vulnerability — Summary for Policymakers" (Geneva: United Nations Environment Programme, 2007). Articles included Ian Smith, "Quarter of Land Mammals and a Third of Those at Sea are at Risk of Extinction," the *Guardian*, October 7, 2008, 13; Andrew C. Revkin, "Arctic Melt Unnerves the Experts," *New York Times*, October 2, 2007, D1; Randolph E. Schmid, "All World's Seas Show Damage," *Toronto Star*, February 15, 2008, A19; Sarah Lyall, "Warming Revives Flora and Fauna in Greenland," *New York Times*, October 28, 2007, 10; Allen Salkin, "Before It Disappears," *New York Times*, December 16, 2007; Kenneth Chang, "Study Finds New Evidence of Warming in Antarctica," *New York Times*, January 22, 2009, A6; Ariana Green, "Asian Beetle Spells Death For Maples So Dear," *New York Times*, November 28, 2008, A25; "Earth on the Brink of an Ice Age" *Pravda* (online), January 11, 2009 (*http://english.pravda.ru/science/earth/106922-0/*).

Chapter Eight

Vancouver's Olympic sustainability program is described in "Vancouver 2010 Sustainability Report Snapshot 2006–07."(Vancouver Organizing Committee for the 2010 Olympic and Paralympic Winter Games, 2006). A critical perspective was provided in Brian Hutchinson, "Coming Clean at Games: Vancouver Olympics Downgrades from Carbon Neutral to Carbon Responsible," *National Post*, May 17, 2008, A7. The impact of climate change on winter sports is covered in Rolf Burki, Hans Elsasser, and Bruno Abegg, "Climate Change and Winter Sports: Environmental and Economic Threats, (Fifth World Conference on Sport and Environment, Turin, 2–3, December 2003); Utah Harnischfeger, "As Alps Warm, a Snow-Deprived Ski Resort Sells for $1," *New York Times*, January 22, 2008, A4; Matt Higgins, "A Season Melts Away: Ice Fishing Industry is Hurt by Unseasonably Warm Temperatures," *New York Times*, January 10, 2007, C16; Thalassic Srikanthan, "Pining for Snow Days," *Toronto Star*, December 28, 2006, A6; Elizabeth Rosenthal, "How Do You Ski if There Is No Snow?" *New York Times*, November 1, 2007, C3; Mark Landler, "Global Warming Poses Threat to Ski Resorts in the

Alps" *New York Times*, December 16, 2006; Haig Simonian, "Thin Falls Make for Slow Going in the Snow Business," *Financial Times*, December 9–10, 2006; Patrick Lang, "Alpine Ski Season Faces Meltdown Because of Global Warming," *National Post*, October 28, 2006; Patrick White, "Home-Ice Advantage," *Globe and Mail*, February 15, 2008, L1; Leslie Scrivener, "On Melting Pond," *Toronto Star*, November 19, 2006, A7; John Tagliabue, "At Dutch National Pastime's Top Event, Mother Nature Wields the Starting Gun," *New York Times*, February 26, 2007, A4; John Tagliabue, "Skaters Rush to Icy Canals in a Rare Deep Freeze that Warms the Dutch Soul," *New York Times*, January 16, 2009, A10; Leslie Garrett, "Ski Resorts Peak at Turning Green Into White Stuff," *Toronto Star*, 15 November 2007, T2. Information on construction of refrigerated facilities at the Vancouver Olympics was presented at the ASHRAE Toronto Chapter meeting on January 5, 2009, by David Sinclair of Cimco Refrigeration.

Chapter Nine

Sources for information on indoor facilities was based on web-based accounts from the United Kingdom, Finland, and Dubai. These include Ski Dubai, SnOasis, BBC UK, World Resources Institute Archives, Greenpeace Archives, *www.winterolympics2026.com*, Vancouver 2010 Sustainability, the *Huffington Post*, and the *Atlanta Journal-Constitution*. In addition, information on new indoor tunnel cross-country skiing facilities was provided by the Toronto Chapter of the American Society of Heating, Refrigeration and Air-Conditioning Engineers (ASHRAE).

INDEX

ABOUT THE AUTHORS

Darryl Humber is the author of two books of fiction. He studied English and semiotics at the University of Toronto's Victoria College. During his studies, he worked two years for the student-run newspaper, *The Strand*, as its sports editor and writer.

He spent his childhood in Bowmanville, Ontario, and currently lives in Toronto, where he is usually found at the ballpark for Toronto Blue Jays home games, or, if the team is out of town, he makes use of Toronto's parks for playing tennis, volleyball, ultimate Frisbee, and soccer.

He has worked with professional baseball organizations, law schools, and currently works in the not-for-profit sector with the United Way.

This is his first writing collaboration with his father.

William Humber is the author of ten books, including *Bowmanville*, and his most recent, *A Sporting Chance: Achievements of African-Canadian Athletes*. His research has earned him induction into Saskatchewan's Baseball Hall of Fame, and the Black Ice Hockey and Sports Hall of Fame in Dartmouth, Nova Scotia. As well he was awarded a Queen Elizabeth II

Photograph by Aleks Janicijevic

Golden Jubilee Medal in 2002 for his community leadership.

Like Darryl, he is a graduate of Victoria College at the University of Toronto, and has a masters in environmental studies from York University.

He has worked as an education administrator at Seneca College for over thirty-two years in the areas of community outreach, continuing education, engineering technology, and is currently developing a major Great Lakes–based institute for the restoration of built and natural environments.

He lives in Bowmanville, Ontario, with his wife, Cathie, where they are occasionally visited by their three children, Bradley, Darryl, and Karen.

Also by William Humber

Bowmanville:
A Small Town at the Edge
978-1-896219-21-9 / $16.95

This is an extraordinarily detailed, often affectionate and occasionally critical account of a modern small town on the edge of a rapidly expanding metropolitan region. The book recounts stories from the time of Charles Bowman, the potential ambition of railroads from Lake Ontario to Georgian Bay, the legacy of grand pianos found in every corner of the world and the fateful decision of a rural businessman that gave General Motors to another community.

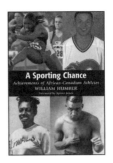

A Sporting Chance:
Achievements of
African-Canadian Athletes
978-1-89621-999-9 / $22.95

Over the years, Canadians have smugly asserted their country's more tolerant culture in race relations. Yet as this story of African-Canadian participation in sports demonstrates, the record is far more troubling. In reality, Canada's record in matters of race was a disturbing blend of occasional good intentions and ugly practices. The study of the Black athletic experience in Canada is not only a revealing portrait into our past, but also one more demonstration of some time-honoured truths about human achievement and the necessity of the public will to provide open and fair forums for equal access to participation.

Of Related Interest

Ebb and Flow:
Tides and Life on Our Once and Future Planet
by Tom Koppel
978-1-55002-726-6 / $26.99

Tides have shaped our world. They have carved out shorelines, altered the course of human civilization, and provided us with the potential for an alternative source of energy. Tides frustrated Alexander the Great and Julius Caesar, and aided General MacArthur. Tides even affect the way our planet moves, and are the reason only one side of the moon faces the Earth, and why eventually only one side of the Earth will ever face the moon.

 **DUNDURN PRESS**
www.dundurn.com   Available at your favourite bookseller

Tell us your story! What did you think of this book? Join the conversation at www.definingcanada.ca/tell-your-story by telling us what you think.

Marquis Book Printing Inc.

Québec, Canada
2009